Afro-Latinx Digital Connections

Reframing Media, Technology, and Culture in Latin/o America

Afro-Latinx
Digital Connections

Edited by Eduard Arriaga and Andrés Villar

UNIVERSITY OF FLORIDA PRESS

Gainesville

First cloth printing, 2021
First paperback printing, 2025

30 29 28 27 26 25   6 5 4 3 2 1

Library of Congress Cataloging-in-Publication Data
Names: Arriaga Arango, Eduard, editor. | Villar, Andrés, editor.
Title: Afro-Latinx digital connections / edited by Eduard Arriaga and
    Andrés Villar.
Other titles: Reframing Media, Technology, and Culture in Latin/o America.
Description: Gainesville : University of Florida Press, 2021. | Series:
    Reframing Media, Technology, and Culture in Latin/o America | Includes
    bibliographical references and index.
Identifiers: LCCN 2020046384 (print) | LCCN 2020046385 (ebook) | ISBN
    9781683402046 (hardback) | ISBN 9781683402398 (pdf) |
    ISBN 9781683405429 (pbk.)
Subjects: LCSH: Social justice—South America. | Social justice—Caribbean
    Area. | Blacks—South America—Social conditions. | Blacks—Caribbean
    Area—Social conditions. | Digital media—South America. | Digital
    media—Caribbean Area. | Racism—Caribbean Area. | Racism—South
    America.
Classification: LCC HM671 .A39 2021 (print) | LCC HM671 (ebook) | DDC
    302.23/1—dc23
LC record available at https://lccn.loc.gov/2020046384
LC ebook record available at https://lccn.loc.gov/2020046385

University of Florida Press
2046 NE Waldo Road
Suite 2100
Gainesville, FL 32609
http://upress.ufl.edu

UF PRESS
UNIVERSITY
OF FLORIDA

GPSR EU Authorized Representative: Mare Nostrum Group B.V., Mauritskade 21D, 1091
GC Amsterdam, The Netherlands, gpsr@mare-nostrum.co.uk

Contents

Abbreviations

CENESEX	Center for National Sex Education (Cuba)
CNOA	Conferencia Nacional de Organizaciones Afrocolombianas (National Assembly of Afro-Colombian Organizations)
IAF	Inter-American Foundation
ICT	information and communications technology
IDB	Inter-American Development Bank
IO	international organizations
IT	information technology
MERCOSUR	Mercado Común del Sur (Southern Common Market)
MINTUR	Cuban Ministry of Tourism
OAS	Organization of American States
PAIGC	Partido Africano da Independência da Guiné e Cabo Verde (African Party for the Independence of Guinea and Cape Verde)
SEGIB	Secretaría General Iberoamericana (General Secretariat for Ibero-America)

Introduction

EDUARD ARRIAGA AND ANDRÉS VILLAR

This book about Afro-Latinx digital connections seeks to highlight how Latin American and Caribbean people of African descent, or Afrodescendants, use digital tools to bolster the agency of individuals and communities, both locally and across national boundaries. Many of the texts collected here are written by academics; interest in digital technologies, however, exceeds the boundaries of the academy, as anyone living in our contemporary connected world can attest. We have therefore also included interviews with Afrodescendants who use digital technologies to foster connections within and among Afrodescendant communities. The technologies examined here are symptomatic of a digital network encircling the globe at a truly breathtaking speed, a network which is itself the result of numerous interwoven networks of different sizes. Developments in mobile technologies, artificial intelligence, and the so-called internet of things are paving the way into a future of even greater human integration with computational hardware and software. Yet compared to the seemingly unalloyed enthusiasm that technology elicited just a few decades ago, today we are more ambivalent about the implications of a digitally connected world. On the one hand we cherish the apps on our phones and the gadgets that seem to make our life more "convenient," but on the other hand we are also increasingly aware that the ubiquity of digital technologies facilitates hacking, the proliferation of malware, and surveillance by state actors and others who can use these same technologies for nefarious ends. Nevertheless, between the poles of utopian freedom of action and dystopian disciplinary control lie other possibilities for individuals and groups to take advantage of what "the digital" has to offer.

Where does all this take us in terms of Afro-Latinx digital connections? We begin with the seemingly self-evident observation that the pervasiveness of digital technology has profound implications for the ambiguous yet inescapable constellations that constitute Afro-Latin America, or Afrodescendant "cultures" (we will address these terms in more detail below), and "cultures" at large, in the broad, anthropological sense of the word. We suggest that this is only seemingly self-evident because although digital technologies are an inescapable feature of daily life, their effect on cultural practices is not always obvious, even though manifold changes make themselves felt on the surface. What is important, however, is to move beyond mere appearances and enact a "deep description" that might give us some indication of how structures inherited from the past, particularly in Black communities, endure or change as digital tools are mobilized. It is important to note that we understand the digital domain not merely as a layer added to a "real" and robust culture that underlies it, much in the way that icing lies on a cake.[1] Rather, the digital is understood as firmly embedded in the practices of everyday life. Wherever digital technologies have been adopted, which is just about everywhere on Earth, the digital has been or is being incorporated into the cultural DNA, so to speak. This is particularly evident in the adoption of the mobile phone (cellphone, smartphone, pocket computer, or however one might want to understand it), which as it has spread across the globe has had large and frequently unforeseen effects on commerce, social relations, and political events. Positing the existence of a digital domain is therefore more an analytical strategy than an ontological one: the digital domain is not, in itself, a discrete and bounded set of objects, rules, and procedures operating at a distance from people and matter, although some of its objects such as hardware and software are commonly imagined that way. Even a cursory forensic examination of all things digital quickly uncovers connections to bodies, geographies, and resources, connections of which the Afro-Latinx digital ones are a subset.

It is also important to note that the digital devices and the infrastructures that make them useful depend on raw resources obtained from many regions of the globe, and that the myriad processes of extraction, production, distribution, usage, and disposal associated with digital technologies have deleterious effects on the environment, as is increasingly clear in our time of environmental emergencies.[2] For example, the labor needed to create and maintain digital devices and keep the digital economy afloat consists of real people, many of whom live in deplorable conditions.[3] We hear about blood diamonds, but how many of us know about the hidden workers that scan texts for Google or Microsoft or that disassemble the components of so-called e-waste?[4] Or how many of us are aware of the people who work according to stringent schedules in the warehouses from where objects purchased online are delivered?[5] Real, concrete matter is at the core of all digital interactions, including at the level of electronic zeros and ones and the surfaces on which they are registered. The digital world, therefore, is material all the way down.

The above digression into what the digital entails might seem tangential to the articles in this book. We suggest, however, that the materiality of digital technologies should be at the forefront of any examination of Afro-Latinx digital connections, lest current issues and claims (social, territorial, economic, environmental, etc.) with long historical trajectories grounded in physical circumstances get lost in the seeming intangibility of the digital domain. Moreover, an overemphasis on immateriality as the essence of the digital can accentuate the age-old division between mind and matter, or between theory and practice, rendering some of the problematics we address here as literally "academic."

Afro-Latin America, Afrodescendant, and Afro-Latinx

The panorama briefly sketched above, much of it now widely discussed in the media and in academic circles, forms part of the frame in which Afro-Latinx digital connections take place. Another critical part of the frame is the well-known history of cruelty and injustice endured by Africans and their descendants in the Americas.[6] Moreover, despite the backbreaking labor they endured (labor that propelled a modernity fueled by commodities such as sugar and cotton), most of these peoples' histories remain absent in national narratives written after the independence movements of the early nineteenth century. People of African descent have been largely erased as actors in the project of nation-building in the Americas, a problematic state of affairs that remains mostly unchanged. It is against this history of invisibility that the terms "Afro-

Latin America," "Afrodescendant," and "Afro-Latinx" have emerged as signifiers of the agency of Black people in the Americas.

"Afro-Latin America" was coined at some point during the 1970s, and, as George Reid Andrews notes, the term was appealing because it suggested a set of common concerns or issues shared by people of African descent across the Americas.[7] This was important at the time, since Blacks were conceived of as a disconnected plurality, even within national boundaries: "Latin American writers and intellectuals had long been referring to their fellow citizens of African ancestry as Afro-Brazilians, Afro-Cubans, Afro-Venezuelans, and so on; from this usage the concept of a larger, transregional category of Afro-Latin Americans followed naturally. To the best of my knowledge, however, no one before [Anani] Dzidzienyo and [Pierre-Michel] Fontaine had thought to transform plural Afro-Brazilians or Afro-Cubans into a singular Afro-Brazil or Afro-Cuba, let alone an all-embracing Afro-Latin America."[8]

This new, broader conception of an Afro-Latin America had momentous implications: "Latin Americans who are Africans" describes a set of individuals subsumed in a larger "Latin America," which is constructed as normative, whereas the term Afro-Latin America suggests a large-scale community with shared concerns, claims, histories, and memories that resist being subsumed under and occluded by the unhyphenated category "Latin America." In other words, "Afro-Latin America" stresses connections across the hemisphere that help define and bolster the agency of a particular set of individuals and groups as well as the connections that allude to a deep historical memory concealed like the bulk of an iceberg beneath the surface of national histories as they have been built in the Americas.

Another important term we have already introduced is "Afrodescendant," which we will use to denote membership in the African diaspora that includes Afro-Latin America as one instance of a complex network of communities and identities, and that, much like "Afro-Latin America," alludes to a set of shared historical circumstances and concerns. "Afrodescendant" has already been adopted by the United Nations, government agencies in various countries, and a growing number of NGOs, an action which is symptomatic of a contemporary momentum in the Black diaspora that is expanding ideas inherent in the concept of Afro-Latin America.[9] The categorical implications of these two terms are not meant to downplay regional differences or needs that are specific to particular places. Rather, the acknowledgment of an overarching historical consciousness and agency of Afrodescendant peoples is an important corrective to an enduring racism and underplays the diverse roles these communities and individuals have played in Latin America.

The third term in the title for this section, "Afro-Latinx," is of relatively recent vintage, and with its related term "Latinx" has added new dimensions to how Afrodescendants and Latin America are conceptualized. For example, historical Afrodescendant claims concerning civil rights continue to be important, but Afro-Latinx digital initiatives have drawn attention to two important issues that have not been sufficiently examined in the past: the role of gender in fashioning Black identities, and the idea that humanity can be defined solely in terms of adult males and females. "Afro-Latinx" has broadened the range of what it means to be Black in Latin America, and the intersectional implications of this term suggest a nuanced creative tension with the overarching category of Afrodescendant, a tension that can counter any temptation to ascribe a determinate positivistic essence to Blackness. We have therefore used the term Afro-Latinx in the title of this book as an acknowledgment of the breadth, variety, and complexity of contemporary Afro-Latin America.

The emergence of Afrodescendant issues in the Americas as described above should not be read as the arrival of agency where there had been none. Like other subaltern groups, such as Indigenous peoples, Afro-Latin Americans have been actively present as historical actors during and after the colonial period. However, the structural categorization of race inherited from colonial times has "edited out" this presence in histories, politics, culture, and the economy, occluding or downplaying the ways Afrodescendants have participated in different social spheres. In turn, Afrodescendants have resisted such concealment and erasure so as to reveal how processes of hegemonic cultural imposition do their work. Maroon communities, which were created by runaway slaves to establish collective ways of being in the world, are notable examples of how Black subjects made themselves visible by resisting bondage.

This tension between the visibility and invisibility of African descendants is the result of particular models of reality whose inbuilt prejudices have had disastrous consequences for millions of Black people. Such models were configured according to discrete rules that qualified data and justified particular actions, skewing representations of the social world and justifying egregious forms of behavior. Residues of these models persist, even in the digital realm, in discourses and representations of Afrodescendant peoples in the Americas.

Scientific racism played a part in these models that rendered Afrodescendants invisible in the histories of the nascent and maturing Latin American republics, but this process was challenged by social organizations, political parties, and worker unions that constantly reinstated the presence and agency of Afrodescendant subjects. In such adverse circumstances, however, Black subjects who wanted to climb the social ladder either downplayed their African heritage or tried to conceal it, bolstering a narrative that Afrodescendants were "peacefully and successfully integrated into national society, ceasing to exist as a separate, identifiable, and, therefore 'visible' social group."[10] Being visible in particular ways involved being invisible in others, and the whole dynamic of resistance and political engagement has continued to develop and be challenged along such an equivocal trajectory.

With this history of social invisibility in mind, this collection of essays and interviews seeks to highlight how Afrodescendant communities in the Americas are adopting and adapting digital tools to form new, varied, and fluid forms of self-representation. The digital strategies described in this book are taking place in a connected world dominated by large companies, a world that is very different from the radically democratic digital one that seemed to be augured by the early internet.[11] The texts collected here, however, show that Afrodescendants in Latin America use digital tools in creative ways within or against powerful currents of economic, scientific, political, and discursive orders, rendering visible the complex legacies of being Afrodescendant in the Americas.

We will use the term Afro-Latinx throughout the volume to name a space of interconnections and shared experiences of racism and discrimination. In particular, and as proposed by Arriaga in his chapter, the term Afro-Latinx will be associated with processes of resistance, creativity, and activism that are enhanced by the power of digital connections. Afro-Latinx includes national attachments, social circumstances, languages, genders, and racial dimensionalities, but it also goes beyond all these categories. In particular, Afro-Latinx speaks of complex relations, affective solidarities, and a continual process of identity maroonage in order to escape and subvert the "machine"[12] that has adopted endless forms throughout history: the slave ship, the plantation, the colonial state, and today the algorithmic determinism of digital technology that quantifies people and in doing so makes them less-than-human, especially people of color or those who live at the margins.

The following chapters are connected by two overarching topics. The first is the relation between notions of Blackness and transnationalism, a relation that is exemplified by the emergence and consolidation of regional and global Afrodescendant identity networks. This is a subject that has been examined in academic, social, cultural, political, and economic discussions about the implications of inclusiveness and recognition. The second topic is the "digitization" of knowledges and know-hows, particularly when these challenge established epistemologies and the channels through which knowledge is distributed, such as educational institutions, media outlets, and state agencies.

Much of the work produced on the relationship between Blackness and transnationalism focuses on the traffic of people, ideas, and things across the Atlantic region. A well-known example of such scholarship is Paul Gilroy's book *The Black Atlantic: Modernity and Double Consciousness*, whose title refers to a concept first proposed by W. E. B. Du Bois to examine how Black cultures emerge out of complex transnational, transregional, and transatlantic relations.[13] Du Bois originally coined the term "double consciousness" to describe a state in which Black individuals experience a "sense of always looking at one's self through the eyes of others, of measuring one's soul by the tape of a world that looks on in amused contempt and pity."[14] In this context, ideals of equality, freedom, and fraternity are informed by a teleological conception of modernity that excludes Afrodescendants and other non-Europeans, who are relegated to the margins by the socio-cultural signifier of race, which fuels colonial projects and constructs social hierarchies in what Walter Mignolo has termed the "darker side" of modernity.[15] Black transatlantic studies have undoubtedly shed light on these issues and made important theoretical contributions to the study of Blackness; however, the emphasis on the North Atlantic region of Europe and North America has tended to downplay the African diaspora in other regions and to overlook what recent studies of colonialism and decolonization have termed "alternative modernities" or alternatives to modernity.[16]

The concept of transnational Blackness that emerges in the following essays goes beyond the double, dialectical consciousness proposed by Du Bois and developed by Gilroy. What we encounter in these pages is a transnational consciousness that, like the African diaspora itself, is a complex network without a single center or dominant geographic location.[17] The focus of the book is Latin America and the Caribbean, but the texts are written with an awareness that the people in this vast geography are connected in meaningful ways to each other and to other Afrodescendants around the world. One can see the effects of these connections in Brazil, Colombia, and the United States, which together account for the largest percentage of Black people outside the African continent. In these three countries, the diverse conceptions of what it means to be an Afrodescendant are intertwined in many ways (symbolically, politically, economically, etc.), facilitating the exchange and dissemination of images, symbols, and ideas used to construct Afrodescendant "ethnoscapes."[18] This traffic of people and ideas across countries and continents has also stimulated notions of transnationalism that move beyond models of a North-South colonial legacy narrated in terms of national histories. This does not mean that nations-as-such disappear, as is evident in categories such as Afro-Colombian, Afro-American, Afro-Peruvian, among others, but rather that nation-states are one point of reference in a constellation that includes other comprehensive categories, such as Afrolatino/a, Afrolatin@, and Afro-Latinx.

Digital Tools, Digital Connections, Digital Humanities

Any examination of how digital tools are being used has to consider the question of access to the relevant technologies. In general, Afrodescendant populations in Latin America confront widespread issues of economic, social, and political inequality on a daily basis, including inadequate access to what the digital age has to offer. One of the aims in compiling this book, however, was to show that Afrodescendant communities are using what is at hand to create, reconfigure, and sustain meaningful connections. That is, we sought to highlight Afrodescendant individuals and communities as being active, rather than passive; as having agency, rather than lacking it. There is no doubt that Afrodescendants in the Americas have been victimized, but stressing this above all else perpetuates a vicious circle that keeps them at the margins of cultural, economic, and political processes.

Questions of agency and the building of connections across the African diaspora have long been studied by authors who approach writing as a technology of communication, but the arrival of digital technologies has created powerful new ways of disseminating information that need to be studied with expanded methods. In addition to providing novel ways to produce and disseminate information, digital media have also made us reassess how we think of culture, identity, and representation, and even of how we construe space and time.[19] Because of this, and because digital media can also displace the loci of enunciation, describing Afrodescendant cultures in the digital age is a complex task. The contributions to this collection give a sense of such complexity by showing how digital tools incorporate "pre-digital" dynamics immanent in Afrodescendant communities in order to enhance collective ties and enact political agendas that can sometimes be at odds with "digital capitalist" interests. This tension, and the sometimes ambivalent encounter between people and digital technologies, affects how the historical claims and identities of Afrodescendant individuals and communities are reconfigured in the present.

A central concept in this book is that of connection, a fundamental component of networks at all scales, from the complex meshwork of our brains to the social relations of our highly globalized world. Connections make a system dynamic and have multiple effects on its evolution and behavior. One can see this in the human brain, which is a dense network of neurons that among many other things helps us learn and use language by connecting experience and memory.[20] All types of networks share characteristics, some of which are surprising: for example, social media has taught us that we are only two or three clicks away from any person linked to our social network.[21] In turn, social media, computers, and big data are linked to the more ancient connections born in the brain and extended through language and culture into the bonds that define human communities. Connections, and the networks they form, therefore have multiple dimensions that implicate objects, ideas, people, and other living things. Afro-Latinx digital connections are no exception: contemporary Afrodescendant individuals and communities in the Americas are using the intermeshing of cultural and digital networks to fight erasure and promote agency. Moreover, the digital technologies help amplify relations that existed long before the advent of digital technologies and without which Afrodescendant communities and identities could not have persisted into the present.

An example of an empowering, critical approach to digital technologies is the emergence of categories such as Afrolatin@ and Afro-Latinx, which are concepts informed by processes of migration, ethnic classification, transnational interconnections, and affirmative representations of Blackness and African descent that resist traditional patriarchal and binary gender identifications.[22] Digital tools—blogs, Tumblrs, *Instagram* pages, and other social media platforms—have played a critical role in giving these terms wider currency in conversations about race, ethnicity, and representation. As a result, notions of Blackness have expanded by promoting alternate epistemological systems and previously unheard-of relationships that are now fundamental for understanding ethno-racial-gender struggles in the digital age. In addition, digital platforms have permitted people who identify as Afrolatin@ or Afro-Latinx to think about new ways of organizing and representing data, such as expanding the categories used to identify gender or race in census questionnaires and other means of gathering information.[23]

The growth of the so-called digital humanities since the early 2000s has also expanded Afrodescendant theoretical discussions by highlighting the intersection of technology, race, gender, and class. This development has coincided with new digital initiatives by people from different epistemological, cultural, and ethnic/racial backgrounds who also challenge the idea that the digital domain is neutral, objective, non-racial, genderless, and classless. A result of these critiques has been the emergence of the so-called Black digital humanities, which have drawn attention to the what the "humanities" in the term "digital humanities" can or should mean.[24] Some examples of work being produced in this area are *eBlack*, which is an ongoing digital resource affiliated with the University of Illinois that was developed by Professor Abdul Alkalimat in 2008; *Technicolor: Race, Technology, and Everyday Life* (2001), a collection of essays edited by Alondra Nelson, Thuy Linh N. Tu, and Alicia Headlam Hines; *Digital Diasporas: A Race for Cyberspace* (2009), a book by Ana Everett; "Black Code," a special issue of the journal the *Black Scholar*, edited by Jessica Marie Johnson and Mark Anthony Neal (2017); "Slavery in the Machine," a special issue of the journal *Archipelagos*, edited by Jessica Marie Johnson (2019); and *New Digital Worlds: Postcolonial Digital Humanities in Theory, Praxis, and Pedagogy* (2019), written by Roopika Risam. The growing support from research centers, institutions of higher education, and funding agencies linked to academic institutions (libraries, research centers, professional associations, etc.) has expanded the reach of the digital humanities and stimulated more of such scholarship.[25]

Despite its grounding in higher education, or because of it, the still-amorphous and ill-defined field of the digital humanities has given rise to concerns about the inclusivity of the "human record" and a search for methodologies and tools that can promote diversity.[26] Teju Cole has noted that traditional Western conceptions of Africa, Africanness, and Blackness are at odds with Western notions of technology, the future, and innovation: Africa suggests images of primitivism, essentialism, and tradition, the opposite of what technology is supposed to embody.[27] Therefore, a change from "grass skirts" to "glass skirts," to use Teju Cole's evocative metonyms for African technology and culture, will represent a radical transformation of how Africa is imagined in the West.[28]

Inclusivity, however, is a much more complex problem that requires more than merely countering such stereotypes. Epistemological diversity, for example, is a more fundamental issue that, because of cultural and infrastructural issues associated with cultural development, will require a more critical and concerted effort to achieve real inclusivity. Johanna Drucker has suggested that a "positivistic, strictly quantitative, mechanistic, reductive and literal" digital humanities is limited in what it can explain.[29] The diversity of cultural manifestations that originate in different epistemologies, as is the case with Afrodescendant communities, requires a more expansive, qualitative reflection not only about what digital technologies might make more transparent but also about what they might render more opaque. The important issue of racial bias in the digital humanities is being addressed in different ways, yet the implications run deeper than the mere color of the skin, since what is needed is a rethinking of the nascent field's practices and basic conceptions so that other epistemologies can be incorporated.[30] In this context, what Jessica Marie Johnson and Mark Anthony Neal refer to as the field of Black Code studies seeks a more radical approach to digital culture and a much more expansive notion of what digital humanities should include. In particular, they note that Black Code "centers black thought and cultural production across a range of digital platforms, but especially social media, where black freedom struggles intersect with black play and death in polymorphic and polyphonic intimacy."[31] Black Lives Matter is perhaps the best-known example of how the convergence of these issues erupts into social action by using digital connections to challenge Afrodescendant erasure. The point to keep in mind in terms of Afro-Latinx digital connections is the suggestion that thought and cultural production are dispersed across a wide array of digital media, which is indeed a formidable and transformative challenge to the traditionally sacred halls of knowledge and the violent apparatuses of social and racial inequality.

This distributed power of thought and cultural production enabled by the convergence and networking of digital technologies has also been used in Latin America to create stronger social connections and generate action around particular issues. Perhaps one of the best-known cases is the so-called Zapatista uprising in Yucatán, Mexico, which took full advantage of the internet's reach to draw worldwide attention to what was happening in the region.[32] Sometimes Latin American digital initiatives have been connected to multilateral, transnational, or private funding agencies with geopolitical interests in the region, such as USAID and the Ford Foundation.[33] This does not imply that people using digital tools or receiving aid from these agencies have been passive receptors who imitate or blindly adopt practices from "developed" countries. In fact, and as the examples in this book show, digital tools and methodologies are being used in multiple ways to challenge the large-scale "market" of production and consumption that excludes most Afrodescendants in Latin America and whose consequence is an oligopolistic geopolitics of knowledge with dire consequences for Black and other subaltern populations.

Digital developments, however, have not been wholly antagonistic or driven by dichotomies such as North vs. South, primitivism vs. civilization, or center vs. periphery. Discussions about the interweaving of race and digital technology have been more varied and multifaceted. Moreover, ongoing developments in technology and artificial intelligence have shifted some emphasis in the digital humanities from digital collections and canonical works toward "physical computing" as a means of stimulating critical thinking and promoting social justice.[34] This is a process that has been going on for some time in Latin America, where technologies are adapted to fulfill particular needs.[35]

Outline of the Book

The editorial impulse for this book proceeds from the so-called digital humanities, but the chapters that follow examine a broad range of interventions, eliciting important questions that are relevant to many fields of inquiry. In particular, this volume follows the line of a digital humanities as digital practice (DHdp), which comprises creative processes that challenge "institutional structures connected only to grant-seeking projects with university affiliation."[36] Our aim, therefore, is to showcase the "polymorphic and polyphonic intimacy," to use Johnson and Neal's phrase, of connections used by Black peoples in the Americas, whom we refer to as Afro-Latinx, as they interact with the digital and innovate within the "machine" so as to disrupt and transform it. To emphasize the fact that knowledge comes in many forms, we have interspersed essays and interviews throughout the collection.

In the first essay, "Afro-Latinx Digital Cultures: Toward Complex and Diverse (Digital?) Humanities," Eduard Arriaga examines how Afro-Latinx communities and individuals are using digital tools to express more inclusive conceptions of humanity, to connect with other communities, and to rewrite traditional histories. Arriaga questions the boundaries of the digital humanities and other scholarly practices and the limited conception of humanity that resides at their core. Arriaga proposes that contemporary Afro-Latinx digital projects be understood as alternatives to, or extensions of, the digital humanities and other digital scholarly projects that aim to expand conceptions of humanity (humanities) and question the contemporary geopolitics of knowledge production. Arriaga's essay contributes to ongoing discussions about the digital humanities and issues of diversity, which have been stimulated by the work of scholars such as Amy Earhart, Tara McPherson, Marisa Parham, Jessica Marie Johnson, and Roopika Risam, and by projects such as Design for Diversity at Northeastern University.

The interview that follows Arriaga's chapter is with Silvana Bahia of Preta-Lab, a digital initiative in Brazil, which is the country with the largest population of Afrodescendants outside Africa itself. The PretaLab exemplifies how Afro-Latinx connections work in locations such as the favelas in Río de Janeiro or Salvador de Bahia, where communities use digital tools to enhance community knowledge and create opportunities, especially for Black women. Bahia stresses how PretaLab is both a lab and a maker-space where Black women adapt digital tools to re-program their role in the digital industry and in Brazilian society.

The next chapter's interview with Afro-Cuban blogger Sandra Abd'Allah-Álvarez Ramírez, stresses the importance of Afro-Latin American and Afro-Caribbean organizations established by women and illustrates how these organizations have created global alliances and audiences across national boundaries.[37] Abd'Allah-Álvarez Ramírez describes her experience with digital technologies and reflects on how her digital practice has helped her understand the global connections among Afro-Latinx women's initiatives as a form of Afro-digital activism. Doing as much as possible with scarce resources, Abd'Allah-Álvarez Ramírez uses minimal computing to overcome digital-capitalist constraints in order to establish Afro-digital feminist connections.[38]

Sandra Abd'Allah-Álvarez Ramírez is also one of the subjects of Maya Anderson-González's essay about the Afro-Cuban blogosphere. In this chapter Anderson-González describes how bloggers such as Abd'Allah-Álvarez Ramírez and Yasmín Silvia Portales Machado have created intersectional practices that examine Latin American culture and re-inscribe Afrodescendant women into Cuban history and the burgeoning Cuban and Latin American world of digital practices. Such a re-inscription of forgotten groups and identities, concludes Anderson-González, becomes part of the identity politics and construction of collective memory in twenty-first-century Cuba, where tradition and history are being called into question in the digital realm.

The next interview is with Mónica Carrillo, an Afro-Latinx affiliated with the NGO Centro de Estudios y Promoción Afroperuanos LUNDU (Center for Afro-Peruvian Studies and Advancement) and Proyecto Afrolatin@ (from New York). Carrillo describes the way Afro-Latinx activists and artists have been creating digital projects to fight racism and to search for social justice at the local, national, and regional levels. Such projects include the Observatorio Afroperuano, which is devoted to the analysis of Peruvian media and its role in the dissemination of racism and racial stereotypes. With little access to tools when it started in 2001, Observatorio Afroperuano resorted to pen-and-paper techniques to perform discourse analysis that eventually had an effect on national policy and social behavior. Carrillo also discusses several experiences from her career as a digital artist, digital activist, and Afro-Latinx digital feminist, revealing how digital media and digital platforms strengthened existing networks and established connections with other anti-racist struggles across the globe.

In "International Organizations Theory and Online Afro-Latin America," Yvonne Captain uses IO theory to demonstrate how small and mid-size organizations survive in online environments that reward digital corporatization based on a greater quantity of links, even at the expense of "racial" or "ethnocultural" interests. Captain suggests that although digital tools have been used to foster cultural, political, and economic agendas, organizations survive and thrive on the internet only if their leaders establish or stimulate a large number of connections.

The interview with Yancy Castillo and Dora Inés Vivanco from the NGO Conferencia Nacional de Organizaciones Afrocolombianos (CNOA, National Assembly of Afro-Colombian Organizations) highlights the coexistence of digital initiatives and analog activism in Colombia. This organization has been using digital tools to connect with Afro-Colombian audiences and highlight their historical, cultural, and political claims. In addition, digital approaches employed by the organization have allowed them to practice a digital activism that includes groups such as women and children, which have generally been overlooked in traditional claims by Afrodescendant communities and other stakeholders.

The next chapter, titled "Toward the Creation of an Afro-Argentine Digital Archive in the Cape Verdean Association of Buenos Aires" and authored by María Cecilia Martino, documents how a group of Afro-Argentinians are reconstituting their collective historical memory. Martino's essay examines an archive created by a Cape Verdean community organization in Buenos Aires that is documenting Afrodescendant individual and collective histories and establishing transnational and transcultural connections. The archive aims to highlight the presence of African peoples in Argentina by making pictures, letters, and other documents available to a wider audience. The creation of the archive and the digital and analog connections it facilitates are important means for this particular Afrodescendant community to intervene in the Argentinian history of race and identity politics.

The interview with the Afro-Colombian cultural promoter and activist Alí Majul shows how Afrodescendant communities in Cartagena are adopting and adapting digital tools to promote intersectional social justice and alternative decolonial representations. Majul uses projects such as the African Film Festival or Afro-Women in the Periphery to showcase how digital tools can connect Afro-Colombian communities. He is critical, however, of activists and other actors who use these same tools to extract local knowledge and use it in venues disconnected from the communities that produced it. Like Abd'Allah-Álvarez Ramírez in the Cuban blogosphere, Majul uses digital gadgets borrowed from people on his social and activist networks to pursue minimal-computing activism.

The last interview in the book features Adebayo Adegbembo, the main designer and digital artist for Genii Games Yoruba101, a start-up based in Nigeria that uses digital tools and platforms to foster Yoruba cultural traditions. This interview takes us to Africa and might seem superfluous in the context of Afro-Latinx digital connections. However, Adegbembo notes that his encounter with Brazilian people and culture has had an effect on his vision of the African diaspora. Furthermore, Adegbembo understands that digital tools can produce diverse representations of humanity, promote positive visions of Africa that counter its image as backward and unwilling to engage with technology, and establish connections with Afrodescendants in other parts of the globe. In all of this, Adegbembo's practice reiterates an expanded notion of Blackness to which the varied and complex expressions of Afro-Latinx identities are inextricably linked.

The final chapter is an epilogue that recapitulates some of the important topics that emerge throughout the book and explores what the case studies collected here might suggest for future research. In particular, it emphasizes how Afro-Latinx digital connections are facilitating a re-examination of established histories and discourses that can set the stage for better and more inclusive futures.

Acknowledgments

Our deepest thanks to our contributors, a group of talented, innovative, and passionate scholars, activists, and practitioners who constantly defy machines and technologies that threaten their existence and those of their communities. We would also like to thank Stephanye Hunter and the editorial team at UFP for trusting our work and supporting its development from the very beginning, nurturing an idea into a full-fledged book. We are grateful for the manuscript readers' generous and thorough feedback, which was invaluable in providing our research and practice with new perspectives and helping refine the project into its present shape. Many thanks also go to the series editors, Juan Carlos Rodríguez and Héctor Fernández L'Hoeste, who were—and continue to be—advocates for research such as ours.

A project of this kind would not have been possible without the support of institutions and people such as the University of Indianapolis, particularly the College of Arts and Sciences; Dorothy Odartey-Wellington, to whom we owe much for believing in this project even before it was a reality; colleagues and mentors—too numerous to name and credit here—who have been allies in our search for knowledge since our student years; and finally, the close relations who are always there for us, willing to support and discuss our work and, more importantly, to infuse it and our life with the love and solidarity that we hope make their way into our writing.

We have kept in mind that the digital, as the texts in the book will show, is very much grounded in both materiality and territoriality. In that sense, it is important to acknowledge that these pages were compiled by the editors on the unceded territories and traditional lands of the Kiikaapoi, Miami, Anishinabek, Haudenosaunee, Lūnaapéewak, and Attawandaron peoples. Finally, let us also acknowledge the ancestors who defied technologies of oppression and who walk and fight alongside us in order to fulfill dreams of a better future.

Notes

1. Lev Manovich has suggested something like this. See Manovich, *Software Takes Command*.

2. For example, see Robinson, "E-waste."

3. See Scholtz, *Uberworked and Underpaid*.

4. See Robinson, "E-waste."

5. See McClelland, "I Was a Warehouse Wage Slave"; and Cadwalladr, "My Week as an Amazon Insider."

6. Texts that are useful entries in the long history of African slaves and their descendants, and other Black communities and people of color, in Latin America are George Reid Andrews's books *Afro-Latin America, 1800–2000* and *Afro-Latin America: Black Lives, 1600–2000*.

7. George Reid Andrews has written that he first encountered the term "Afro-Latin America" in articles of the late 1970s by the political scientists Anani Dzidzienyo and Pierre-Michel Fontaine. Andrews, *Afro-Latin America, 1800–2000*, 3–4.

8. Ibid.

9. The issue of African descent was made current by the 2001 World Conference against Racism in Durban, South Africa, and more recently by the United Nations' declaration of 2011 as the International Year of People of African Descent. Eduardo Restrepo has called the widespread, international adoption of the term "Afrodescendant" the "Durban effect." Restrepo, "Articulaciones de negridad," 155. The term "Afrodescendant" itself, however, seems to have been coined at a conference in Chile in the year 2000, and if this is the case it would have originated in "Afro-Latin America." Díaz, "Afrodescendientes en la construcción de diálogos entre Venezuela y África," 88–89.

10. Andrews, *Afro-Latin America, 1600–2000*, 4.

11. The negative implications of digital media present new challenges of a different order. See O'Neil, *Weapons of Math Destruction*, 18.

12. See Johnson, "Markup Bodies."

13. Gilroy, *The Black Atlantic*.

14. Du Bois, *The Souls of Black Folk, 8*.

15. See Mignolo, *The Darker Side of Western Modernity*.

16. See Gaonkar, *Alternative Modernities*.

17. The adoption of the "International Decade for Peoples of African Descent" by multilateral agencies such as the UN is another example of attempts to define transnational Blackness

and unify experiences that may have common roots but are nevertheless expressed in too many ways to be contained comfortably within one neat category.

18. The term "ethnoscapes" was coined by Arjun Appadurai. See Appadurai, *Modernity at Large*.

19. Taylor and Pitman, eds., *Latin American Identity in Online Cultural Production*, 2–3. See also Manovich, *The Language of the New Media* and Manovich, *Software Takes Command*.

20. See Presti, *Foundational Concepts in Neuroscience*.

21. Stanley Milgram's 1967 study of social networks in the United States gave rise to the idea of a "six-degree separation," although more recent studies have shown the connections in most networks to be even closer than that. Albert-László Barabási describes Milgram's experiment and other developments about networks in Barabási, *Linked*, 27–30 and 38–39; for Milgram's original study, see Milgram, "The Small World Problem."

22. Rivera-Rideau and Paschel, *Afro-Latin@s in Movement*.

23. Those tools could be digital or analog. What really matters is that they are developed and grounded in particular cultural and epistemological ways to interpret the world.

24. See Gallon, "Making a Case for the Black Digital Humanities."

25. Salient examples of digital projects from higher education that examine race are Digital Schomburg at the New York Public Library; Digital Harlem; African American History, Culture and Digital Humanities; Soweto 76 Archives; and the Colored Conventions Project.

26. One of the current initiatives is the Design for Diversity group at Northeastern University, which is "focused on the ways in which information systems embody and reinforce cultural norms."

27. See Cole, "Do African Digital Natives Wear Glass Skirts?"

28. Ibid., 39–40.

29. Burdick et.al., *Digital_Humanities*, 43.

30. For critiques of racial bias, see McPherson, "Why Are the Digital Humanities So White?" and Gallon, "Making a Case for the Black Digital Humanities."

31. Johnson and Neal, "Introduction," 1.

32. Cleaver, "The Zapatista Effect"; for other examples of Latin American activism and the internet see Sorj and Fausto, *Activismo político*.

33. Initiatives such as Alfabetizaciones digitales from the Centro de Memoria Histórica in Colombia were funded by USAID. Unfortunately, the traces of these connections are disappearing due to political and ideological changes experienced in the region, under the lead of the US. However, it is still possible to see some connections that were much more visible six to eight years ago. See "Memorias del Conflicto." Likewise, initiatives such as Instituto Mídia Étnica in Brazil, as well as CNOA in Colombia, examined in Arriaga's chapter in this volume, have been developed with funds from the Ford Foundation. See "Proyectos," CNOA, and Correio Nago, a social media platform designed by the Instituto Mídia Étnica.

34. Physical computing is a term that encompasses various hands-on practices with hardware and software. Arduino is one of the better known and popular ways in which a particular idea of physical computing has become widespread. Physical computing, however, also encompasses diverse strategies to use available materials to create custom-made computer systems, whether by choice (as in DIY culture) or by necessity. See Syers et al., "Between Bits and Atoms" and O'Sullivan and Igoe, *Physical Computing*.

35. Eduard Arriaga's chapter in this book provides examples of physical computing

born of necessity as computer technology is adapted to local conditions of knowledge or infrastructure.

36. Johnson, "4DH + 1 Black Code/Black Femme," 666.

37. As the author of *Negra Cubana Tenía Que Ser* and a member of *Afroféminas*, Sandra Abd'Allah-Álvarez Ramírez has contributed to this phenomenon.

38. Minimal computing is the use of computers "under some set of significant constraints of hardware, software, education, network capacity, power, or other factors." Its advocates understand it as "a critical movement, akin to environmentalism, asking for balance between gains and costs in related areas that include social justice issues and de-manufacturing and reuse, not to mention re-thinking high-income assumptions about 'e-waste' and what people do with it." "About," Minimal Computing.

Bibliography

"About." Minimal Computing, accessed March 10, 2020. http://go-dh.github.io/mincomp/about/.

Andrews, George Reid. *Afro-Latin America, 1800–2000*. Oxford: Oxford University Press, 2004.

———. *Afro-Latin America: Black Lives, 1600–2000*. Cambridge, MA: Harvard University Press, 2016.

Appadurai, Arjun. *Modernity at Large: Cultural Dimensions of Globalization*. Minneapolis: University of Minneapolis Press, 1996.

Barabási, Albert-László. *Linked: The New Science of Networks*. Cambridge, MA: Perseus Publishing, 2002.

Burdick, Anne, Johanna Drucker, Peter Lunenfeld, Todd Presner, and Jeffrey Schnapp. *Digital_Humanities*. Cambridge, MA: MIT Press, 2012.

Cadwalladr, Carole. "My Week as an Amazon Insider." *Guardian*. December 1, 2013. https://www.theguardian.com/technology/2013/dec/01/week-amazon-insider-feature-treatment-employees-work.

Cleaver, Harry M. "The Zapatista Effect: The Internet and the Rise of an Alternative Political Fabric." *Journal of International Affairs* 51, no. 2 (1998): 621–40.

Cole, Teju. "Do African Digital Natives Wear Glass Skirts?" *Journal of the African Literature Association* 11, no. 1 (2017): 38–44.

Correio Nago. http://correionago.ning.com/.

Design for Diversity, Northeastern University Library, https://dsg.neu.edu/research/design-for-diversity/.

Díaz, Diógenes. "Afrodescendientes en la construcción de diálogos entre Venezuela y África." *Humania del Sur* 7, no. 12 (January–June 2012): 79–94.

eBlackCU. Accessed February 28, 2020. http://eBlackcu.net/portal/introduction.

Everett, Anna. *Digital Diaspora: A Race for Cyberspace*. Albany: State University of New York Press, 2009.

Gallon, Kim. "Making a Case for the Black Digital Humanities." In *Debates in the Digital Humanities 2016*, edited by Matthew K. Gold and Lauren Klein. Minneapolis: Minnesota University Press, 2016.

Gaonkar, Dilip Parameshwar, ed. *Alternative Modernities*. Durham, NC: Duke University Press, 2001.

Johnson, Jessica Marie. "4DH + 1 Black Code/Black Femme Forms of Knowledge and Practice." *American Quarterly* 70, no. 3 (September 2018): 665–70.

———. "Markup Bodies. Black [Life] Studies and Slavery [Death] Studies at the Digital Crossroad." *Social Text 137* 37, no. 4 (December 2018): 58–79.

———. "We Are Deathless (Slavery in the Machine)." *Archipelagos*, no. 3 (July 2019). https://archipelagosjournal.org/issue03/guest_editors_intro.html.

Johnson, Jessica Marie, and Mark Anthony Neal, eds. "Black Code," special issue of *Black Scholar* 47, no. 3 (2017).

———. "Introduction: Wild Seed in the Machine." *Black Scholar* 47, no. 3 (2017): 1–2.

Manovich, Lev. *The Language of the New Media*. Cambridge, MA: MIT Press, 2001.

———. *Software Takes Command*. New York: Bloomsbury, 2016.

McClelland, Mac. "I Was a Warehouse Wage Slave." *Mother Jones*, March/April 2012. https://www.motherjones.com/politics/2012/02/mac-mcclelland-free-online-shipping-warehouses-labor/.

McPherson, Tara. "Why Are the Digital Humanities So White? or Thinking the Histories of Race and Computation." In *Debates in the Digital Humanities*, edited by Matthew K. Gold. Minneapolis: Minnesota University Press, 2012.

"Memorias del Conflicto." http://www.memoriasdelconflicto.com/index.php/las-minas-de-hiracal/item/46-las-minas-de-hiracal-1985–2010.

Mignolo, Walter. *The Darker Side of Western Modernity: Global Futures, Decolonial Options*. Durham, NC: Duke University Press, 2011.

Milgram, Stanley. "The Small World Problem." *Psychology Today* 1, no. 1 (May 1967): 61–67.

Nelson, Alondra, Thuy Linh N. Tu, and Alicia Headlam Hines, eds. *Technicolor: Race, Technology, and Everyday Life*. New York: New York University Press, 2001.

O'Neil, Cathy. *Weapons of Math Destruction: How Big Data Increases Inequality and Threatens Democracy*. London: Penguin Books, 2017.

O'Sullivan, Dan, and Tom Igoe. *Physical Computing: Sensing and Controlling the Physical World with Computers*. Mason, OH: Course Technology, 2010.

Presti, David E. *Foundational Concepts in Neuroscience*. New York: Norton & Company, 2016.

"Proyectos." CNOA. https://convergenciacnoa.org/proyectos/.

Restrepo, Eduardo. "Articulaciones de negridad: Políticas y tecnologías de la diferencia en Colombia." In *Hegemonía cultural y políticas de la diferencia*, edited by Alejandro Grimson and Karina Bidaseca, 147–63. Buenos Aires: CLACSO, 2013.

Risam, Roopika. *New Digital Worlds: Postcolonial Digital Humanities in Theory, Praxis, and Pedagogy*. Evanston, IL: Northwestern University Press, 2018.

Rivera-Rideau, Petra, Jennifer A. Jones, and Tianna S. Paschel, eds. *Afro-Latin@s in Movement*. New York: Palgrave Macmillan, 2016.

Robinson, Brett H. "E-waste: An Assessment of Global Production and Environmental Impacts." *Science of the Total Environment* 408, no. 2 (December 20, 2009): 183–91.

Scholtz, Trebor. *Uberworked and Underpaid: How Workers are Disrupting the Digital Economy*. Cambridge, UK: Polity Press, 2017.

Sorj, Bernardo, and Sergio Fausto, eds. *Activismo político en tiempos de internet*. São Paulo: Plataforma Democrática, 2016.

Spence Brown, Devyn. "What Is Afro-Latin America?" Black Perspectives, African American Intellectual History Society, September 4, 2016. https://www.aaihs.org/what-is-afro-latin-america/.

Syers, Jentery, Devon Elliott, Kari Kraus, Bethany Nowviskie, William J. Turkel. "Between Bits and Atoms: Physical Computing and Desktop Fabrication in the Humanities." In *A New Companion to Digital Humanities*, edited by Susan Schreibman, Ray Siemens, and John Unsworth, 1–21. Oxford, UK: Wiley Blackwell, 2016.

Taylor, Clare, and Tea Pitman, eds. *Latin American Identity in Online Cultural Production*. New York: Routledge, 2013.

1

Afro-Latinx Digital Cultures

Toward Complex and Diverse (Digital?) Humanities

EDUARD ARRIAGA

An increasing number of digital projects and initiatives carried out by Afrode-scendant communities in the Americas (North, Central, and South America and the Caribbean) make us reconsider the boundaries and limits of what has been known as the digital humanities. Although the field has experienced a continuous expansion to accommodate diverse perspectives, discussions are still ongoing about what the digital humanities are and should be, especially when dealing with groups outside of academia that have had a different relationship to knowledge creation and dissemination and therefore use digital tools and platforms in ways that differ from communities in academic or professional fields. This essay will contribute to those discussions by analyzing the way Afro-Latinx[1] communities make use of digital technologies' inherent potentials, questioning not only the digital as a medium but also pursuing projects that aim to reinstate humanity to subjects from which it has been historically denied.

Although digital technologies and dynamics (digitization, visualization, data mining and data analysis, etc.) have been increasingly presented since the 1990s and early 2000s as neutral, transparent, and useful tools with which to achieve democracy, justice, and equality, the present text departs from such generalizations in order to understand how diverse communities interact with digital tools that are understood as cultural artifacts. In fact, following scholars such as Safiya Umoja Noble, Ruha Benjamin, Cathy O'Neil, and Jacqueline Wernimont, among others, this essay considers such tools and dynamics as cultural artifacts that carry values and biases and therefore have effects on the ways humans connect, represent, and interact.

Likewise, this essay expects to overcome a limited conception of a "digital divide" as merely a lack of access to tools and technologies due to economic, cultural, and social barriers.[2] It is clear that at a certain point, hardware and software that enabled people to get connected to the digital world and become part of the "knowledge economy" were expensive and hard to access by marginal communities and individuals, but that is not the case with an array of technologies in our current digital ecosystem. For example, smartphones and other tools that are part of the so-called internet of things have allowed more people to access digital capabilities. As proposed by Anita Chan in her book *Networking Peripheries*, the hype from technological centers and the narratives these centers create and disseminate make us forget how "processes of innovation and histories of experimentation have also come in from the edges."[3] Unfortunately, such expansion does not come at a low price: access or the lack thereof to the logic and the algorithms behind those widespread devices has created a wider divide between the people who make digital tools and those who consume them. In addition, making digital tools increasingly accessible has opened the door for corporate producers to gather and exploit users' data without much control, affecting the way users manage, transmit, and present their own information to the world. That is, the relationship between the digital world and the communities and individuals who participate in it must continue to be seen as "constituted in terms of mediating culture."[4] Some of the projects and initiatives analyzed here show how Afro-Latinx communities are aware of those divides and how they adopt tools to create their own representations and to understand the opacity generated by algorithms (cultural artifacts) that operate within digital tools.

Another divide that arises in discussions and implementations of digital tools in marginal contexts is that between the Global North and the Global South. Afro-Latinx communities and individuals find common ground in the use of digital tools as a way to amplify and connect with communities from diverse contexts and locations with which they share struggles and experiences. Although contextual and situational differences are fundamental for understanding how these communities appropriate and use digital tools, many of their projects evoke shared experiences of resistance and creativity. Roopika Risam has rightly argued that all good practices in digital humanities are local practices,[5] meaning that the imposition of a centralized conception of digital humanities would overlook the context as a fundamental component to understand diverse conceptions of humanity and the digital. In the case of the digital projects I have been investigating, it is the productive interconnection between local digital practices and transnational shared experiences of marginalization that have allowed the creators of those projects to use digital tools critically to create new worlds in which diverse humanities are re-centered, speaking back to exclusionary narratives in both the humanities and the innovation sector. Whether examining farmlands in Colombia, Brazil, or the United States, or examining police brutality as a state strategy of control in urban settings, such Afro-Latinx projects make use of data, information, and digital analysis to make visible complex conceptions of humanity. Moreover, such projects use digital tools to blur geographical and regional differences, fostering instead alternative epistemologies in which human and non-human entities are in constant interconnection.[6]

Afro-Latinx: Interconnected Blackness in the Americas

Afro-Latinxs have been seen from diverse and sometimes contradictory perspectives. They have been considered transnational subjects, whose complexity in terms of history, politics, and social relations positions them as mediators of realities and social issues that affect more than one set of the population. They have been construed as communities and individuals who have been invisible or at the margins of "both African American and Latino histories."[7] Finally, they have been examined through the exclusive and exclusionary condition of categories such as Afrolatin@s, Afrolatinxs, or Afro-Latin Americans, which by definition limits them to Spanish-speaking Black communities. This leaves other Black communities out of the conversation—for example French-, Portuguese- and English-speaking Black communities formed by migration flows from and to the Caribbean.[8] In any case, when speaking about Afro-Latinx as a category, we are constantly referencing a dynamic space not only of local histories and global experiences of race, racism, discrimination, but also of processes of creativity, resistance, and resilience. When referencing Afro-Latinxs and Afro-Latin Americans, we are calling attention to communities and individuals of intermingled racial and ethnic identities that determine their political, cultural, and social position in the contexts in which they act. With shared aspects in their histories of colonialism, discrimination, and exclusion, these communities and individuals develop processes of creativity, re-invention, and re-creation in order to question current epistemological visions from intersectional perspectives that vary depending on the context.[9]

The processes of re-creation and re-invention of cultural and racial identities in the Afro-Latinx communities have been developed through diverse media: oral traditions, writings, music, and still images, among others. These and other elements have been constantly used to make communities and individuals visible and to promote legal, political, and activist actions that have prompted a concrete understanding of how these communities and individuals are interconnected. However, in the past decade the adoption of digital media has emerged as an important way not only to make visible the aforementioned complexity, but also to connect communities and realities that were not previously considered related or sharing common histories and experiences. Other media, as well as the representations they convey, have been directly affected by the way digital technologies add new symbolic layers to cultures that are complex in nature. Additionally, these technologies have permitted alternative ways to read, represent, and self-represent those racial and cultural identities.

If a range of representations has permitted imagining Afro-Latinx communities as interconnected, it is important to start thinking about how this has been affected by the digital turn. It is clear that connectivity has been constantly presented as one of the most important characteristics and benefits of digital technology, with such connectivity having an impact on diverse social discourses an actions. However, few studies have focused on the adaptations, adoptions, and interactions of those communities with new technologies of interconnection.[10] In that sense, "Afro-Latino and Afro-Latin American studies not only need to expand and include each other as a way to capture the trans-border nature of their subject of study," but they also need to embrace those new symbolic layers added by the adoption of digital discourses and practices.[11] This will allow us not only to account for the already complex racial, geographical, and political relations of the communities under study, but also to understand how digital technologies and dynamics are changing, and will continue to change, the way Afrodescendants in the Americas produce knowledge, represent their own identities, claim rights, and interact with society as a whole. Issues such as data appropriation and analysis and algorithmic activism become fundamental for understanding how these communities are grappling with historical challenges that are reshaped by new technologies and dynamics. Engaging in these discussions and creating frameworks to understand the debates about Afro-Latinx digital cultures will be of importance to secure a genuine decolonization and to understand how the multifaceted conception of Blackness in the Americas has emerged from interconnections that it is currently strengthening in novel ways.

Afro-Latinx Digital Cultures: Beyond (Black) Digital Humanities

In their volume *Digital_Humanities*, Anne Burdick, Johanna Drucker, Peter Lunenfeld, Todd Presner, and Jeffrey Schnapp argue that "digital humanities is an extension of traditional knowledge skills and methods [from the humanities] and not a replacement for them."[12] Presented in such a fashion, the digital humanities is supposed to continue the work of the humanities but in digital contexts and under the limits and affordances of digital technologies. In that sense, the digital turn of the humanities makes humanists "confront questions of worth, cultural significance, deeper meaning . . . the nature of knowledge, the world as a human construction as well as the human ability to establish understanding with various degrees of certainty" through digital capabilities that have deeply affected the way those questions are approached and researched.[13]

The field of the digital humanities has gradually expanded in the last few years, opening the door to work on racial, national, and cultural differences, providing a way to bridge the gap created by traditions of erasure and discrimination long denounced by critical approaches. However, as Lev Manovich has argued, the digital humanities created its own domain in relation to the type of data scholars in this field study, analyzing mostly historical artifacts created by professionals and whose temporal scope is under the frame allowed by copyright laws. In that sense, "digital humanists shut themselves out from studying the present."[14] Users who do not claim any expertise but create digital pieces that might or might not be considered art, or those who want to challenge the "Man-as-Human"[15] conception of humanity to re-inscribe cultural, racial, or gender identities through the use of digital expressions, tend to lie outside the scope of the humanities and the digital humanities. Such is the case for Black communities in the Americas that, because of historical circumstances, need to recover what was stolen or to re-invent what was erased or made invisible. With that in mind, it is possible to affirm that Afro-Latinx digital projects go beyond the horizon of the so-called digital humanities, due to their complex connection to epistemology, materiality, and temporality, among others.

In making the case for Black digital humanities as an alternative project to that of the digital humanities, Kim Gallon explains that it "might be considered as a digital episteme of humanity that is less tool-oriented and more invested in anatomizing the digital as both progenitor of and host to new—albeit re-lated—forms of racialization."[16] Although Afro-Latinx digital endeavors might be seen as an instance of the project heralded by Gallon, these are broader and expand on epistemological and intersectional grounds. Afro-Latinx digital ini-tiatives might be defined as sets of complex epistemologies based on dynamic interconnections (intersectionality) of race, ethnicity, gender, class, and cul-ture, among others. These kinds of digital humanities projects are networked initiatives connected by common histories of exclusion and by regional com-monalities, linguistic familiarities, or political agendas. However, such con-text-specific elements can hinder attempts to make these projects examples of a "digital episteme of humanity," to use Gallon's words. Moreover, Gallon's proposal belongs to a context in which racial discussions have been detached from discussions of class and colonial/political oppression and presented as independent and therefore disconnected from other levels of human experi-ence.[17] However, she recognizes such a separation in her proposal and consid-ers Black digital humanities an attempt to achieve those missing connections.

Afro-Latinx digital projects may be seen as overcoming these gaps as they pursue similar issues to those proposed by Gallon for the Black digital hu-manities. Afro-Latinx initiatives examine race as represented by phenotypic expression through color and the cultural implications of Blackness as a global phenomenon. However, the scope of their initiatives supersedes these issues by connecting diverse racial, cultural, economic, gender, and other elements in frameworks informed by the circumstances of colonialism and imposition faced by diverse Black communities in the Americas and beyond. All of these elements impinge on racially tinged conditions constructed as natural for so-called Third World communities, even in the heart of the Global North.

Authors such as Safiya Umoja Noble, Roopika Risam, and Babalola Titilola Aiyegbusi, among others, have pointed out how the digital humanities have supplanted—and in the worst cases excluded—racialized and diverse ethnic visions in the name of universalized conceptions of the digital and the cultural human record.[18] In addition, Noble uses the case of Jarret Drake, a former digital archivist at Princeton University, to argue for a more committed digital humanities that is less concerned with digitality and the computerization of literary and cultural documents and more attentive to the pressing issues faced by society in general but particularly by people of color. Noble claims that "the digital humanities can profoundly alienate Black people from participating in its work because of its silences and refusals to engage in addressing the intersecting dimension of policy, economics and intersectional racial and gender oppression that are part of the society we live in."[19] These proposals go beyond a mere process of recovery as heralded by Kim Gallon's Black digital humanities and focus more on showcasing how Black communities have agency to claim their own versions of humanity through what I have called "digital maroonage,"[20] understood as a cultural practice that uses the digital to develop counter-hegemonic processes to defy orders that have dehumanized Black subjects.

Afro-Latinxs, who are overwhelmingly forced to live doubly marginalized lives, present themselves as more connected with political struggles and alternative social projects that aim to defend human life and humanity as a whole. In this sense, many of the projects complement Gallon's vision of the Black digital humanities by creating alternative digital actions. Such projects are alternative with respect not only to the digital humanities or other academic fields, but also to economic, cultural, and political agendas that belong to dehumanizing social orders. Moreover, this constant process of creativity and re-invention assumes that human beings are complex and relational, which challenges anthropocentrism and emphasizes the bonds between human and non-human entities as fundamental for our existence. In fact, these projects and initiatives are more in tune with what Jessica Marie Johnson calls "Black Code," which is rooted in the endless "challenge of living in the wake of Black people rendered in-human, non-existent and disposable by the slave-ship, the plantation, the colonial state, the prison, the border."[21] The digital turn, from the perspective of many users who have been excluded or objectivized, becomes yet another space that amplifies such unresolved social and human issues.

Without taking away from African American traditions and legacies, Afro-Latinxs are beginning to confront the single-dimensional projects of color identity and to incorporate ethnicity, gender, class, and other elements that make the discussion much more complex. Continuing the legacy of Afro-Latin American and Caribbean social movements that, at the end of the twentieth century and the beginning of twenty-first century, called global attention to issues faced by African descendant communities globally, Afro-Latinxs digital initiatives have attempted to bridge divisions created by neoliberal globalization and the globalization of Blackness as a commodity. Their aim is social justice and the defense of the human condition, not as a characteristic exclusive to or represented by the professional creators mentioned by Manovich and whose data is so precious to the humanities, but as processes that evolve thanks to continuous interactions with particular territories, with other human and non-human beings, and with systems of communication and classification. Finally, it is important to clarify that although Afro-Latinx digital projects have been developed with diverse conceptions of Blackness in several locations through the Americas, they always have the idea of making explicit Afrodescendants' humanity as a condition that has historically been denied by colonial powers but achieved and re-invented by rebellious and creative actions.

Afro-Latinx digital projects' search for the recognition of Afrodescendants' humanity does not have to do with asking for acceptance into what Sylvia Wynter has characterized as the "Man-as-Human" Eurocentric conception of humanity. On the contrary, those initiatives not only try to resist or criticize such a conception, but they also propose alternative visions of humanity that are connected to territory and to other conceptions of the economy, society, and human interactions. If, following Mignolo and Wynter, we accept that "the Human is the product of a particular epistemology, yet it appears to be (and is accepted as) a naturally independent entity existing in the world,"[22] these projects use their own epistemological systems and complex realities to challenge the epistemology of such an external, universalized human. Through the adoption of diverse media—including digital tools and platforms—these individuals and communities try to disseminate their proposals to other communities; they try to showcase images that were not previously recognized and to promote diverse ways to be human in diverse localities.

In her article "Markup Bodies," Jessica Marie Johnson argues that the current proliferation of digital approaches—including those that see themselves as advocates for social justice, such as the digital humanities—as well as digital tools and digital structures reproduce and disseminate processes of quantification that can be traced back to slavery.[23] This idea is connected to the "thingification" that Aimé Cesaire proposed as a fundamental characteristic of the relationship between colonizer and colonized through which the humanity of the colonized—usually people of color and inhabitants of the Global South—is put into question. Likewise, Roopika Risam argues that the conception of humanity in the digital humanities, particularly in the context of algorithmic and artificial intelligence, is defined by a universalized conception of a human subject that does not represent or take into account local ways of being human.[24] All this is, in turn, connected to Ruha Benjamin's claim that technology functions not only "as a metaphor for race, but [as] one of the many conduits by which past forms of inequality are upgraded."[25] In that sense, Afro-Latinx subjects and communities do not use digital tools to fit these into an idea of human and humanity that historically has excluded them. They employ these tools and platforms in a process of constant breaking, dancing, and re-inventing,[26] as well as with the idea of promoting the interconnection of diverse ethnicities and races that, despite their diversity, have suffered from the same exclusions and exploitations.

Afro-Latinx Digital Culture

Some of the most interesting projects that take part in what this volume calls "Afro-Latinx digital connections," particularly for the transnational and transregional Afro-Latinx communities, range from what is now considered the basic use of blogs to more complex appropriations of algorithms and digital technologies to produce, intervene, and re-evaluate data. In the same vein, some projects express local concerns and goals, while others have more global aims. Languages and the way technologies are used also play an important part in understanding how these projects unfold and how they get connected to current waves of Black digital activism.

The digital collection *Un caso de reparación: Un proyecto de reparación histórica y humanidades digitales* (A case of reparation: A project of historical reparation and digital humanities) created by Afro-Colombian visual artist Liliana Angulo, one of the few initiatives that explicitly mentions and addresses the digital humanities, is an interesting example of what I have been discussing so far. Using archival research, Angulo explores the Archivo General de Indias (Seville) in order to access historical documents from the Botanical Expedition in the Viceroyalty of New Granada (a colonial administrative region that encompassed modern-day Colombia, Ecuador, and Venezuela). Angulo searches these documents in order to identify Black and Afrodescendant assistants and artists who took part in the expedition but whose contributions have remained in the shadow of the expedition's directors and noblemen. Through her research Angulo not only tries to restore the humanity of enslaved Africans and Afrodescendants by showing how they contributed knowledge and developed visual work, but also to question the way institutions such as the Royal Botanical Gardens of Madrid or the General Archive of the Indies currently make it difficult to discover and access historical accounts about those populations.

Angulo, along with a group of collaborators, is developing a digital collection to shed light on those documents and people that, according to the project's mission statement, were hidden by "the method of naming and classifying created by Linnaeus and used by José Celestino Mutis, the expedition's director."[27] Using digital tools and digital techniques, Angulo has developed a process of re-discovery, re-naming, and re-classification. Created in Altervista—a freemium platform for designing and publishing websites and blogs—*Un caso de reparación* features a simple interface with a tapestry-like background that disappears as soon as the user scrolls down to access another interface, which is divided into two sections: a project description and a gallery with the documents. The description introduces the project by stating its main ideas and conceptions; the gallery shows a section of tags and thumbnails of the documents that were researched and curated to be displayed as part of the collection. The user can click either on the tags to re-organize the documents depending on the tag clicked, or on each of the thumbnails to trigger a pop-up window that contains an image of the original manuscript, metadata (such as an item description, catalogue number, people named in the document, etc.), and a transcription that makes it easier for the reader to understand the texts, which are images of the original manuscripts. The collection is a visual organization of the information Angulo encountered in her archival research and it has one main goal: to make visible what has been hidden or erased by the way history has been told in Colombia and in the Americas in general.

Although Angulo's project is not a history and is not developed by a historian, it uses history to understand the sources—seen here as a master discourse—of current injustices faced by Indigenous and Afro-Colombian communities, injustices that together with the lived environment are fundamental elements of those communities' identities. The sources researched and re-organized through digital means show, Angulo argues, a socio-racial order centered around a model of extractivism in relation to natural species. Such a model was not only applied in that particular expedition, but it directed the development and informs the existence of the national project to this today. The main injustices are the uncontrolled exploitation of natural resources and the displacement/erasure of people and epistemologies that contributed—and continue to contribute—to the consolidation of nations and national projects.[28] In that sense, *Un caso de reparación* is a digital project that highlights the way the Botanical Expedition denied humanity—as represented in artistic actions, in labor, and in social participation—to Afrodescendant enslaved people.

Using what she discovers, along with the power of classification and amplification brought about by digital tools, Angulo contributes to current processes of symbolic and economic reparations. *Un caso de reparación* also helps recognize effective social, cultural, and economic means of participation that Afro-Colombians and Indigenous communities can use to take part in national projects that have failed them and exploited the environment without care or respect for its future. In this case, the digital is used to create alternative projects of social coexistence with human and non-human entities that constitute those complex, previously ignored worlds and to affirm a humanity that goes beyond its Eurocentric conception, universalized by philosophy, art, literature, and other discursive mechanisms. Opposed to "liberal humanism," which is rooted in "the power of the individual, the head of household, Man,"[29] projects like *Un caso de reparación* re-discover a Black humanity centered around the kinship of community and the coexistence of the living and the dead. The project also discloses the seemingly new—because it has been hidden—fundamental interconnection between those long-ignored Black peoples (their descendants) and the Earth.

Another project that uses digital tools to address the issue of reparations is Reparations for Black and Indigenous Farmers, an initiative by Soul Fire Farm, which is a collective of farmers and activists that, among other activities, is engaged in: a) seeding or establishing community food sovereignty, b) uprooting racism in the food system, c) reversing industrial agriculture's damage to the planet, and d) training farmer-activists, particularly Black Latinx and Indigenous farmers. Although its concern is not the use of digital tools per se, Soul Fire Farm resorts to digital platforms and techniques to amplify, connect, and map out activities, actors, and locations connected to active cases of land reparation.

One of the most important digital projects created by the organization is the Reparations for Black-Indigenous Farmers Map. The reparations map uses geotagging and all the affordances of the Google Maps platform to locate resources needed by Black Latinx and Indigenous farmers to grow food responsibly and to use these resources to claim rights and reparations for the centuries of dispossession and discrimination inflicted on them by the food industry. This is an open-source initiative that asks interested participants—who Soul Fire Farm describes as people of color—to list resources, link actors, and make visible similar initiatives that could be useful for new farmers and for ethnic and racial communities interested in farming. The project is developed on the idea that the "food industry was built on stolen land and stolen labor of Black, Indigenous, Latinx, Asian and people of color," and the map is part of the process of reparations, claims, and solidarity through which those farmers look to gain an alternative space in the food industry.[30]

As was the case with the project developed by Liliana Angulo, the reparations map tackles issues of both racial injustice and dispossession of territory. Although the geographical context is the United States (but includes one initiative in the Caribbean), the reparations map project looks to reinstate the humanity of diverse communities of people of color through the use of digital tools. It also stresses connection with non-human entities that help define their humanity: land, food, and territory. In contrast to Angulo's project, this initiative is geared more toward activism and does not use historical documents or archival research to make visible what has been edited out from history; however, the reparations project creates archives and maps of initiatives, proposing a new symbolic layer and therefore a new construction of the real through algorithmic and interconnected technologies. Although the project is immersed in the socio-racial context of the United States, where racial categories are coupled with ethnic ones, the reparations map addresses a wide variety of identities by adopting the term "people of color" and including Black Latinx, Indigenous, and Asian identifications as part of the endeavor. In that sense, the digital connections overcome the limits of both racial and ethnic identities in order to address complex social problems that do not disappear in the so-called digital age.

Memorias del Río Atrato is another project that also explores the links between humans and non-human entities—particularly territories—and the ways digital tools can reinstate or re-invent the humanity of Afro-Latinxs.[31] This may well be considered a spatial humanities project developed by a community in the Atrato region, located on the Pacific coast of Colombia, as a way to tell their stories in connection with their territory. As victims of the Colombian war and violence perpetrated by guerrillas, paramilitary groups, and the army, Afro-Colombians from the Atrato region have been stripped of their humanity through the violation of their rights and the destruction of their identities and environments.

The project was developed by Atrato river communities, which are overwhelmingly Black and Indigenous, with the aid of the National Center for Historical Memory (Centro Nacional de Memoria Histórica).[32] The initiative, in turn, is part of the program Digital Literacies (Alfabetizacones Digitales), a component of a national endeavor to create strong institutions and bolster the agency of the victims of the Colombian armed conflict. The idea of the Digital Literacies program was to train communities and victims of violence in the use of digital tools and platforms. With the support of agencies such as the United Nations and the United States Agency for International Development, these communities started to use digital tools to tell their stories about their own territories and the way they have been affected by the Colombian armed conflict. Armed with smartphones and trained in multimedia storytelling, the communities started to name and therefore to articulate utopias in the form of videos, songs, and oral stories to define their territories and identities.[33]

Although the project is not focused on discussions about race and cultural identity, but rather on memory as a process connected to situations of trauma and violence, it is undeniable that ethno-racial particularities are fundamental to the development of the project and the use of digital tools. The peripheral status of the Atrato region and its communities—geographically, politically, and culturally—makes the Atrato River dwellers very vulnerable to all the harms and threats from the diverse and complex armed actors, which have constantly silenced voices from the region. Memorias del Río Atrato becomes a way for the people of the region to showcase what they see as a possible future for their own lives in connection with complex identities that are in constant construction through their everyday life experiences. Although it is undeniable that Afro-Colombian and Afrodescendant subjects are at the core of the project, this initiative uses digital tools to make visible how humans of diverse ethnicities and races are trying to re-invent their place in the world; in this case, theirs is a place taken by force but re-invented and recovered through narrative and digital storytelling.

Another project, developed by CNOA (the Spanish initialism for the National Conference of Afrodescendant Organizations), is a Colombian network of regional social movements devoted to working with Afro-Colombian communities. The organization's main goals are connected to safeguarding the human rights and the interests of Afrodescendant communities; however, the organization has turned to the use of digital tools as a way to store memories, educate, and reach other communities.[34] CNOA does most of its work in rural areas, where access to digital tools and the expertise to use them is low. To overcome these challenges, the organization has adopted a methodology based on extensive collaboration and sharing of knowledge. What this means in practice is that when CNOA approaches a given community in which the elders and other members do not know how to use or access the digital tools necessary to record information, the organization relies on the more experienced users in the community who do have access and know how to use digital technologies. With limitations of access and expertise in mind, the organization created material devices such as a *caja de herramientas*,[35] or toolbox, to educate Afro-Colombians about their rights and how to defend them. The toolbox is also a useful aid for participating in the digital realm in order to educate, showcase knowledge and culture, and achieve concrete goals related to human rights, issues of discrimination, and the visible enhancement of Afrodescendants as political actors at both the national and international levels.

One of the most important recent projects developed by CNOA is *Leilani*,[36] a digital book of children's stories told by children. The idea of the e-book is to educate Afro-Colombian children about the importance of looking at their own identities with pride. The e-book was the result of creative workshops in which ten Afro-Colombian children took part and later helped create the e-book. With diverse themes such as family, ancestral medicine, self-esteem, and Afro-Colombian diversity, among others, this digital project addresses infancy and childhood as levels of identity that are usually left out of conversations about recognition, racism, and discrimination. In that sense, CNOA fosters digital representations that go beyond the digital and help formulate utopias in which women and children—minorities within minority groups—become protagonists of their own history. Through digitization of oral histories, CNOA wants to make visible the complex humanities that give life to Afro-Colombian communities and which are very different from the single-dimensional and monolithic understanding of race. On the contrary, CNOA proposes a type of digital deconstruction and decolonization of racial politics and actions.

LatiNegrxs Project is another initiative that highlights the way Afro-Latinxs adopt digital tools to showcase their racial, ethnic, gender, and political struggles in countries such as the United States. This initiative uses blogs and basic websites as tools and platforms to amplify LatiNegrxs' goals and connect with other communities around the country and around the world. Its main goal is to develop a space of anti-oppression and support LatiNegrxs equity in access and representation everywhere.[37] As outlined in its mission statement, LatiNegrxs' digital spaces are used to discuss the lived realities and histories of all who identify as racially Black and ethnically Latinx throughout the world, thereby showing awareness of the diversity of identities and the possibilities offered by digital tools.[38]

The LatiNegrxs webpage shows a variety of information, ranging from pictures and videos, as well as articles written by the project's team members and linked from other websites. All these pieces are designed to narrate and make visible diverse representations of Blackness and diverse ways to be Black in contexts of migration and cultural intermingling. However, there are two important elements that stand out: a) innovation in terms of racial/ethnic identity, and b) discussion of gender as fundamental for understanding the complexity of Afro-Latinx identities. The first element is represented in the same word that gives title to their project: LatiNegrxs reflects the complex intersection of issues that informs the everyday lives of Black Latinx individuals and communities. In contexts such as United States, where racial classification has been fundamental in the formation of the society as it is lived today, as well as in the systematic segregation of individuals into groups—whether by means of race, ethnicity, gender, and sexuality, among others—LatiNegrxs becomes a way to deconstruct such rigid categorizations and highlight the fluidity of communities and individuals aided by digital capabilities. In addition, as a concept, the term "LatiNegrxs" reveals an international connection with an African diaspora—not limited to an imagined African continent—that defies the mythology of purity; on the contrary it makes visible the cross-pollination of rich transnational connections with diverse experiences at local levels. Diverse histories come together and affirm that there is not only one way to be Black or Latinx, but many different possibilities can be conveyed by the power of digital tools and other systems of classification.

The second element that stands out about LatiNegrxs is its discussion of gender. The use of the "x" in the plural word "Negrxs" speaks about a focus on the collective that goes beyond the dual division of gender into male and female to include preferences in which racial, ethnic, and other identities intersect. Since LatiNegrxs' mission is to create a space that is against oppression, its project members envision such a space as inclusive in terms of languages (fundamental to the recognition of Afro-Latinx communities), and of gender, sexual, physical, mental, and emotional identities. The best way to include all those forms of existence is through the power of connectivity, simultaneity, and interaction that digital tools possess and that have been so critical for current ways of understanding culture. Thus, people interested in participating in LatiNegrxs and that identify as both Black and Latinx, in addition to other identities, are invited to make their existence as Afro-Latinxs concrete by sending communications, posting, and participating in creating complex representations that by extension also defy conceptions of single and unified Afrodescendant and Latino identities.

Finally, another project can help us understand how digital connections work at transnational, transhemispheric, and transepistemological levels is PretaLab. The lab is an initiative led by Silvana Bahia, an Afro-Brazilian journalist who is part of a social organization, Olabi, that fosters the democratization of technological production and the inclusion of marginal actors in the field of technological innovation. Bahia and her collaborators had the idea of creating a space to map the field of digital technology in Brazil and connect Black women to it. After investigating diverse sources and being part of several collectives, workshops, and initiatives related to the development of start-ups, apps, and code for both corporate and social enterprises, Bahia identified the lack of diversity and representation/participation of Black Brazilians—let alone Black women. In a world ever more centered around digital capabilities, the centralization of digital power in the hands of a few people will result in increasing inequality. Bahia argues that women, particularly Black and Indigenous women, need to be part of the changes brought about by the global economy and technological development if they want to be represented and if they want to help create alternatives to societies centered around white and heterosexual male power.

PretaLab members understand that today's world is managed through data and data analysis. With that knowledge in mind, in 2017 they created a web space and composed a survey to gather concrete data on the way Afro-Brazilian and Indigenous women see, interact with, and participate in the digital world. Thanks to the survey, PretaLab gathered personal histories and data that allowed its members to see in detail the gap in digital access and appropriation by Afro-Brazilian women. The project's main objectives were: a) to make visible the lack of representation of Black women as an issue connected not only with digital technological fields but also with human rights and basic representation of humanity, and b) to foster the development of positive models to inspire Black women to enter fields such as digital technology, engineering, and other spaces of creation and innovation. These objectives were meant to address issues of access, understood not as consumerism but as the possibility for Afro-Brazilian and Indigenous women to participate in and contribute diverse perspectives and epistemologies to the process of production.

The conception of access PretaLab proposes is far from a naive celebration of digital technologies as panaceas for structural problems such as racism, discrimination, and other social injustices. On the contrary, PretaLab members are aware that digital tools and platforms are not neutral and instead carry political, economic, and cultural values infused by their creators and producers—usually white heterosexual rich men.[39] It is up to Black/Indigenous women, transsexual, and marginalized communities to learn how to use these new languages, how to hack the code spread throughout the internet, and how to create their own more inclusive, socially just, and flexible version of the internet, of the digital, and of data about themselves. Thus, PretaLab expects not only to make particular issues visible, but also and overall to address them through what Bahia, citing Paulo Freire, calls a "pedagogy of autonomy" based on the autonomy of Black and Indigenous women and marginalized individuals' right to search for epistemological alternatives to those that condemn such groups to disappear.[40] PretaLab, then, proposes a restoration of the humanity of Black and Indigenous peoples through a "universal human ethics," understood as the ethics that condemns social injustices arising from monolithic truths that discriminate on the basis of race, gender, or class.[41] The digital thus becomes the field of action for these groups, as it is understood not as a space of pure instrumental connections but as a new version of our changing cultures.

Toward an Afro-Digital Connection

The projects presented above are only a small sample of the diverse digital initiatives carried out by Afro-Latinx communities and individuals. As we have seen, the appropriation, adaptation, and use of digital tools by these and other Afro-Latinx individuals and communities have allowed them not only to connect with people around the world, but also to showcase diverse ways to be human beyond the idea disseminated by liberal humanism. A common denominator in most of these projects is the critical perspective from which technology is seen and used. If authors such as Sylvia Wynter questioned the "ethnoclass (i.e., Western bourgeois) conception of the human, Man, which overrepresented itself as if it were the human itself,"[42] these projects question the seemingly self-evident neutrality and transparency of the digital domain and the problematic features it has inherited from a discursive and material modernity. They do so in order to propose alternative epistemologies or systems of classification for knowing and understanding our world and alternative ways to use and re-program digital tools. Likewise, adopting digital tools and platforms critically means engaging with technologies as objects that incorporate values, but more importantly for these projects is using digital tools to have an impact on the systems of values that are behind the construction and implementation of these very same tools. Following Safiya Umoja Noble's proposal for the development of a critical Black digital humanities, these projects go beyond the digitality and computerization privileged by the digital humanities. On the contrary, they adopt the digital as a way to create counter-hegemonic proposals that account for more "immediate, pressing global concerns,"[43] becoming agents of change for issues in which Black and Brown people are usually seen as victims. In that sense, the digital becomes a space through which decolonial and deconstructive approaches are used to present a world with a universal human ethics that respects human beings in all their diversity and that gives everyone better opportunities to live well. Such a space is what this volume has defined as Afro-Latinx digital connections, whose reach and scope go beyond racial and ethnic boundaries to include human, non-human, and posthuman entities.

Notes

1. Although there are diverse concepts and categories with which to talk about Black communities in the Americas and particularly in Latin America, in this essay I will be using the term Afro-Latinx as a way to render the complexity (in terms of race, origin, social class, and gender) from which these communities emerge and interact. Although there are concepts, such as Afro-Latino, Afro-Latin@, or Afro-Latin American, that are sometimes used interchangeably despite reference to diverse historical, geographical, political, and cultural realities, the term Afro-Latinx seems to better represent the interconnections—digital and analog—this volume aims to highlight. Afro-Latinx as a concept showcases the dynamic spaces of local and global histories and experiences of race, racism, and discrimination, as well as the resistance, creativity, and endless adaptation these communities have developed.

2. The discussion of the "digital divide" in the Latin American context has adopted several forms; however, one of the most important discussions was developed around the case of the Zapatistas and their alternative use of the internet and digital tools from the jungle in Mexico. See Pitman, "Latin American Cyberprotest."

3. See Chan, *Networking Peripheries*, xii.

4. Sassen, "Mediating Practices," 109.

5. Risam, *New Digital Worlds*, 143.

6. Achille Mbembe shows how the conversation on modernity is closely connected to the discussion of capitalism, the creation of a system of organization, and the selection of bodies and objects that could be seen as dispensable. See Achille Mbembe and David Theo Goldberg, "Conversation."

7. Castillo-Glasgow, "Afro-Latin@ Nueva York," 143.

8. López Oro, "'Ni de aquí ni de allá,'" 71.

9. André Brock's work with critical technoculture discourse analysis (CTDA) is a good example to understand how Black communities use and appropriate information and communication technologies. Although his work exclusively focuses on African American communities, its methodology and findings can be cautiously connected to the Afro-Latinx and Afro-Latin American experiences. See Brock, "Critical," 1015.

10. McGahan, "Race-ing for Cybercultures," 4.

11. De la Fuente, "Afterword," 292.

12. Burdick et al., *Digital_Humanities*, 16.

13. Burdick et al., 4.

14. Manovich, "The Science of Culture?"

15. Wynter, "Unsettling," 263.

16. Gallon, "Making the Case."

17. Gallon's project may be read as an inheritor of what Achille Mbembe considers the globalization of "the African American archive" and "the Middle Passage paradigm which has dominated the discourse on blackness almost globally." These two paradigms have been fundamental in the invention of the "Black reason" and Blackness, presumably as an "ontological category." See Achille Mbembe and David Theo Goldberg, "Conversation."

18. See Noble, "Toward"; Risam, "Navigating," 359–67; Risam, *New Digital Worlds*; and Aiyegbusi, "Decolonizing," 434–47.

19. Noble. "Toward."

20. Arriaga, "Yolanda Arroayo."

21. Johnson and Neal, "Introduction," 1.

22. Mignolo, "Sylvia Wynter," 115.

23. Johnson, "Markup Bodies," 58.

24. Risam, *New Digital Worlds,* 141.

25. Benjamin. "Catching," 148.

26. This is a play on words inspired by Marisa Parham. See Parham, ".break .dance."

27. Angulo, *Un caso.*

28. Ibid.

29. Johnson, "We Are Deathless."

30. Soul Fire Farm, "Reparations."

31. Unfortunately, the original URL has not been in service since 2017. This shows the fragility of some of these projects when funded by institutions that are not organically connected with the communities. However, the videos and interviews that constituted the bulk of the site reside now on their own YouTube channel "Memorias del Río Atrato." This speaks about the resilience and flexibility of both the project and the community to showcase their processes of digital cultural activism.

32. Centro, "Memorias del Río Atrato."

33. Lombana-Bermudez, "Voices."

34. Conferencia, "¿Quiénes somos?"

35. The toolbox consists of a cardboard box with materials inside, including a CD with information regarding rights of Afro-Colombian communities, as well as possibilities of connection and interconnection through the use of digital platforms. The toolbox is very useful in rural contexts where there is no internet coverage but where the communities have access to electricity and a computer. Even in regions without electricity or computers, the toolbox is an alternative way to create analog connections and share knowledge.

36. Conferencia, *Leilani.*

37. Laureano. "Mission."

38. Ibid.

39. Silvana Bahia, interviewed by the author, April 13, 2018, transcript.

40. Freire, *Pedagogia.*

41. Ibid, 13.

42. Wynter, "Unsettling," 260.

43. Noble, "Toward."

Bibliography

Aiyegbusi, Babalola Titilola. "Decolonizing Digital Humanities. Africa in Perspective." In *Bodies of Information,* edited by Elizabeth Losh and Jacqueline Wernimont, 434–47. Minneapolis: University of Minnesota Press. 2018.

Angulo, Liliana. *Un caso de reparación: Un proyecto de reparación histórica y humanidades digitales.* Accessed on October 10, 2018. http://uncasodereparacion.altervista.org/?doing_wp_cron=1542474609.0070869922637939453125.

Arriaga, Eduard. "Yolanda Arroayo Pizarro o la construcción de un cimarronaje electrónico." *Casa de Las Américas* 267 (April–June 2012): 24–37.

Bahia, Silvana. *PretaLab*. Accessed on July 25, 2018. https://www.pretalab.com/.

Baxter, Miller. Introduction to *Black American Literature and Humanism*. Lexington: University Press of Kentucky, 1981.

Benjamin, Ruha. "Catching Our Breath: Critical Race STS and the Carceral Imagination." *Engaging Science, Technology and Society* 2 (2016). DOI:10.17351/ests2016.70.

Burdick, Anne, Johanna Drucker, Peter Lunenfeld, Todd Presner, and Jeffrey Schnapp. *Digital_Humanities*. Cambridge MA: MIT Press, 2016.

Brock, André. "Critical Technocultural Discourse Analysis." *New Media and Society* 20, no. 3 (2016): 1012–30.

Castillo-Glasgow, Melissa. "Afro-Latin@ Nueva York: Maymie De Mena and the Unsung Afro-Latina Leadership of the UNIA." In *Afro-Latin@s in Movement*, edited by Petra Rivera, Jennifer A Jones, and Tianna S. Paschel, 141–71. New York: Palgrave Macmillan, 2016.

Centro Nacional de Memoria Histórica. "Memorias del Río Atrato." Accessed on October 10, 2018. http://www.centrodememoriahistorica.gov.co/index.php/noticias/noticias-cmh/1663-memorias-del-rio-atrato.

Chan, Anita. *Networking Peripheries: Technological Futures and the Myth of Digital Universalism*. Cambridge, MA: MIT Press, 2013.

Conferencia Nacional de Organizaciones Afrocolombianas (CNOA). *Leilani. Historias contadas por la infancia afrocolombiana*. Accessed on July 15, 2018. https://convergenciacnoa.org/leilani-historias-contadas-por-la-infancia-afrocolombiana/.

———. "¿Quiénes somos?" *Conferencia Nacional de Organizaciones Afrocolombianas*. Accessed on June 10, 2017. https://convergenciacnoa.org/.

De la Fuente, Alejandro, "Afterword: Afro-Latinos and Afro-Latin American Studies." In *Afro-Latin@s in Movement*, edited by Petra Rivera, Jennifer A Jones, and Tianna S. Paschel, 289–304. New York: Palgrave Macmillan, 2016.

Freire, Paulo. *Pedagogia da autonomia*. Sao Paulo: Paz e Terra, Coleção Leitura, 1996.

Gallon, Kim. "Making the Case of the Black Digital Humanities." In *Debates in the Digital Humanities 2016*, edited by Matthew K. Gold and Lauren Klein. Minneapolis: Minnesota University Press, 2016.

Jiménez Román, Myriam, and Juan Flores, eds. *Afro-Latin@ Reader*. Durham: Duke University Press, 2010.

Johnson, Jessica Marie. "We Are Deathless (Slavery in the Machine)." "Slavery in the Machine" issue, *Archipelagos* 3 (July 2019). http://archipelagosjournal.org/issue03.html.

———. "Markup Bodies. Black [Life] Studies and Slavery [Death] Studies at the Digital Crossroad." *Social Text* 36, no. 4 (137) (December 2018): 57–79.

Johnson, Jessica Marie, and Mark Anthony Neal. "Introduction: Wild Seed in the Machine." "Black Code" special issue of *Black Scholar* 47, no. 3 (2017) https://www.theBlackscholar.org/recent-issues/.

Laó-Montes, Agustín. "Hacia una cartografía del campo político afrodescendiente en las Américas." *Revista Casa de Las Américas* 264 (2011): 16–38.

Laureano, Bianca. "Mission & Goals." *LatinNegrxs Project*. Accessed on October 30, 2018. https://lati-negros.tumblr.com/mission%20and%20goals.

Lombana-Bermudez, Andrés. "Voices from the Atrato River." "Displacements." *ReVista. Harvard Review of Latin America* 16, no. 2 (2017): 16–19. Accessed on October 9, 2018. https://docplayer.net/40166931-Winter-2017-harvard-review-of-latin-america.html.

López Oro, Paul Joseph. "'Ni de aquí ni de allá.' Garífuna Subjectivities and the Politics of Diasporic Belonging." In *Afro-Latin@s in Movement*, edited by Petra Rivera-Rideau, Jennifer A Jones, and Tianna S. Paschel 61–85. New York: Palgrave Macmillan, 2016.

Manovich, Lev. "The Science of Culture? Social Computing, Digital Humanities and Cultural Analytics." *Journal of Cultural Analytics*, May 23, 2018. Accessed on October 1, 2018. DOI: 10.22148/16.004.

———. *Software Takes Command*. New York Bloomsbury Academic, 2013.

Mbembe, Achille. "Knowledge and the Question of the Archive." *Wits Institute for Social Change*. Accessed on October 1, 2017. http://wiser.wits.ac.za/event_archive.

Mbembe, Achille, and David Theo Goldberg. "Conversation: Achille Mbembe and David Theo Goldberg on Critique of Black Reason." *Theory, Culture & Society*, July 3, 2018. Accessed October 1, 2018. https://www.theoryculturesociety.org/conversation-achille-mbembe-and-david-theo-goldberg-on-critique-of-black-reason/.

McGahan, Christopher. "Race-ing for Cybercultures: The Performance of Minoritarian Cultural Works as Challenge to Presumptive Whiteness on the Internet." PhD diss., University of New York, 2004.

Memorias del Río Atrato. Accessed on December 10, 2016. http://www.memoriasdelatrato.org/.

———. Accessed April 20, 2020. https://www.youtube.com/user/memoriasrioatrato.

Mignolo, Walter. "Sylvia Wynter: What Does It Mean to Be Human." In *Sylvia Wynter: On Being Human as Praxis*, edited by Katherine McKittrick, 106–24. Durham: Duke University Press, 2015.

Noble, Safiya Umoja. "Toward a Critical Black Digital Humanities." In *Debates in the Digital Humanities 2019*, edited by Matthew K. Gold and Lauren F. Klein. Minneapolis: University of Minnesota Press, 2019. https://dhdebates.gc.cuny.edu/projects/debates-in-the-digital-humanities-2019.

Parham, Marisa. ".break .dance." *Archipelagos. A Journal of Caribbean Digital Practice* 3 (July 2019). http://archipelagosjournal.org/issue03.html.

Pitman, Thea. "Latin American Cyberprotest." In *Latin American Cyberculture and Cyber Literature*, edited by Claire Taylor and Thea Pitman. Liverpool: Liverpool University Press, 2007.

Risam, Roopika. *New Digital Worlds: Postcolonial Digital Humanities in Theory, Praxis, and Pedagogy*. Evanston, IL: Northwestern University Press, 2019.

———. "Navigating the Global Digital Humanities: Insights from Black Feminism." In *Debates in the Digital Humanities 2016*, edited by Matthew K. Gold and Lauren F. Klein, 359–67. Minneapolis: University of Minnesota Press, 2016.

Sassen, Saskia. "Mediating Practices: Women with/in Cyberspace." In *Living with Cyberspace: Technology and Society in the 21st Century*, edited by John Armitage and Joanne Roberts, 109–19. London: Continuum, 2002.

Schomburg, Arthur A. "The Negro Digs Up His Past." "Harlem Mecca of the New Negro" issue of *Survey Graphic* (1925). Accessed on September 3, 2017. https://web.archive.org/.

Soul Fire Farm. "Reparations. Reparations Map for Black-Indigenous Farmers." Accessed on October 2, 2018. http://www.soulfirefarm.org/support/reparations/.

Wade, Peter. "Rethinking Mestizaje: Ideology and Lived Experience." *Journal of Latin American Studies* 37, no. 2 (May 2005): 239–57.

Wynter, Sylvia. "Unsettling the Coloniality of Being/Power/Truth/Freedom: Towards the Human, after Man, Its Overrepresentation—an argument." *CR: The new Centennial Review* 3, no. 3 (2003): 257–37. Accessed on November 1, 2018. https://law.unimelb.edu.au/__data/assets/pdf_file/0010/2432989/Wynter-2003-Unsettling-the-Coloniality-of-Being.pdf.

2

Digital Autonomy and Knowledge Production
by Black Brazilian Women

Interview with Silvana Bahia

EDUARD ARRIAGA AND ANDRÉS VILLAR
TRANSLATED BY EDUARD ARRIAGA AND ANDRÉS VILLAR

This interview features a conversation with Silvana Bahia, director of Olabi, a Brazilian NGO that promotes the democratization of technology and innovation among diverse communities, with a particular emphasis on Afro-Brazilian women. Bahia also directs PretaLab,[1] an initiative mapping the role of women of color in the Brazilian fields of technology and innovation. The conversation highlights Bahia's ideas about technology, digital tools, and knowledge production and dissemination, ideas that challenge the current geopolitics of knowledge production and the digital economy.

* * *

1. How did the idea of PretaLab come to life?

Well, first it is important to say that I am a journalist; my formation is in journalism. However, I have always been interested in the role of new technologies, particularly as means of communication. Since I am a young, thirty-two-year-old woman I feel I get along well with the transition from analog to digital media. I worked for several years in Maré, a complex of favelas in Rio de Janeiro;

I worked for *Observatorio du Favelas* [Favelas Observatory], an organization devoted to the defense of human rights and the study of urban culture. As a journalist, I came to study ways in which the community created channels of communication, and I started to be quite interested in what people do to read the computer's screen. Then in 2014 I participated in and helped produce a programming workshop for women called RodAda Hacker. As part of the workshop, participants were asked to come up with a project or an initiative they want to develop, and my idea back then was the creation of a website for an independent film that I worked on called *Cabello*, whose central theme is the situation of the Black women in Brazil. As part of the RodAda workshop you are assigned a mentor or advisor who gives you instructions and helps you understand programming. My mentor really liked my idea, my project, and she really wanted to help me make that website. She started to teach me more about programming, and I started to understand a bit more about that universe. I never imagined myself programming. I always thought it was a thing that was not for me; I did not know I would be able to program because I was more interested in human rights.

The following year, in 2015, I coordinated six RodAda Hacker workshops in São Paulo with the idea of decentralizing these workshops and making them more accessible. Decentralizing because the content related to technology and innovation is usually connected to privileged places in the city, connected to particular types of people, and women in particular are not represented. At the time, Gabriela Agustini, who is my colleague from Olabi, the organization in which I am currently working, invited me to work with her in the organization. Olabi is an NGO whose main objective is to work toward democratization in the production of new technologies. Our mission is to bring technology and technological content to any type of citizen, to people who do not normally deal with them or do not understand how those technologies work.

In my first year at Olabi I traveled a lot. I went to Colombia and to other places in order to attend events related to technology. I realized that I didn't encounter any women, let alone Black women or men. Finding Black attendees in those events was practically impossible. Then I said, "Wait, I need to do something about this." I needed to do something in order to allow people like me, who come from the place I came from, to come into contact with and experience digital technology. But to experience it not as consumers, because people are always consuming. However, a question that was always there inspiring me was: What would change if those technologies (software, applications, etc.) were thought about and developed by people with different visions, origins, culture, etc.? What changes when Black, LGBTQ, poor, and disadvantaged people think about those technologies? These are the questions that have motivated me and helped me to imagine PretaLab. Then, in late 2016 I thought about what to do to address those issues. At the time, I was thinking of creating an innovation workshop for Black women, in order to exchange knowledge about technology. It was in that particular moment when I started to think about who were the Black women working in that field in Rio de Janeiro; there were only a few of us. I thought it would be a good idea to develop a program with Olabi focused on Black women because that is the problem: although we are few, we do exist; Black women working in technology do exist, and PretaLab is a project that intends to map them. So, I started PretaLab with two main objectives: one was to create a campaign with videos, interviewing women that were discovered by the mapping process. There is an issue here that is at the same time subjective and objective: there are no examples to refer to women working in tech. You do not have other women that came before and are role models for new generations. So this project is working toward that objective as well. At that point, it was important to stress that in this project the notion of technology was considered from a broader perspective. Technology does not only refer to tools and processes with a mathematical base or centered around and produced by engineering. We also started to include in that definition of technology women who make things, women who produce audio visual content, etc.

2. What is the current stage of the project?

At this point, the project is in a stage of analysis of all the data gathered through the interviews and the mapping, understanding that it was not academic research but rather a collaborative and active-participant-research project. People continue gathering information; however, we are currently focused on analyzing all the information that has been collected. People are building a new site to showcase that content. Based on that, we want to understand what area of the technological industry Black women are focusing on. We would also like to know what their main interest is in taking part in that field. Because there are several studies today in Brazil that want to discuss the issue of gender in technology. However, the term "women" is so broad that it may encompass several things. In contrast, when you limit your scope to Black women it changes your focus and the place where you need to search for information. For instance, I have some figures that say that the number of women accepted into technology courses in Brazil is 16%. That number is not bad, but people do not realize that the majority of those 16% are middle-class white women. So, that is precisely the role PretaLab is playing, creating a campaign to point out that people need to talk about the intersectionality of gender and race when the main points at stake are digital technologies of innovation.

3. What are the advantages and drawbacks of the digital tools we have been talking about?

I think that the most important characteristic is the fact of being able to connect with any Black woman around the world. Also, those tools allow us to have models and points of reference with regard to what Black women do anywhere in the world. So I think that what the internet and other technologies brought about was the possibility of seeing yourself in other spaces, and also of connecting with women that take a path similar to yours. On the other hand, I think that those technologies are also very dangerous and violent to women in general, because if in today's society machismo and racism are spread around the world, those technologies reproduce them. That can be changed when people start to produce such technologies with their own values. The majority of these technologies and digital tools are produced by white, heterosexual men, usually from the Global North; they are not produced by people in the Global South, in the world's periphery. Also, it is important to mention that these tools and technologies in general are not neutral, but rather are defined by the values held by those who built them. I am talking not only about social media, but also about data. Because in today's world data are the most precious wealth. Then, although my idea is not that all Black women become programmers, I think they should have some knowledge and understanding of the field everyone is talking about, thinking that there are no Black women in it. But everything is touched by digital technology nowadays: whether through Skype, a cellphone, or even through the trace of data you leave when you purchase something on the internet. My struggle is for women to understand what digital technology is about.

4. You mentioned that technology cannot be reduced to the digital realm.
What else do you consider technology from PretaLab's perspective?

For instance, I consider that there is something I call "social technologies." As an example, here in Brazil the moto-taxi [motorcycle taxi] could be considered as an innovation that is solving a problem in the favelas, in the Brazilian periphery. They solve a problem of urban mobility that governments and traditional institutions have not tackled. They reach places that other means of transportation do not reach. Now, thinking about "social technologies," we have quite an interesting project that I really admire called "data_labe,"[2] a data lab here in the favelas of Rio de Janeiro whose main work is the interpretation of data. I think that this kind of knowledge is a form of social technology. However, here in PretaLab we think that technology is not only digital. For instance, woodworking is a form of technology. For that reason, it is very common here [in the PretaLab] to connect traditional knowledge, such as clothes making and woodworking, with more contemporary digital technology and processes, such as 3D printing, electronics, etc. Here in the PretaLab we have a course entitled "High-Tech Couture" whose main goal is mixing those forms of traditional knowledge with tools that are more high-tech so they can create wearables. It is closely connected to the maker culture, the DIY movement, etc.

5. What are the effects (both positive and negative) of digital technology in
your culture, whether it be local, regional, national, or international?

I think one of the positive effects is the possibility of content creation about favelas, the periphery, etc. That is, we can have new narrators who do not necessarily create all new content, but who showcase new possibilities to be in a world that is sometimes represented as one-dimensional. In that sense, digital technology allows us to create new and alternative spaces, different from those to which we were assigned. Likewise, when we or those new narrators have access to new dimensions, we are also able to invent new technologies—but from a critical perspective—to handle data and analyze it.

With regard to negative effects, I think that when people produce content in a very superficial way they do not realize what occurs behind the scenes. For instance, nowadays people give away lots of information on social media, but they do not really know where those data are going to end. You have noticed that I speak about data, because data is what really influences today's public policy. So if people do not have data or they do not document a particular problem, the problem does not exist. That is why the PretaLab wants to map the existence of Black women in technology to show that there is a problem. Without data, it is as if the problem does not exist. At the same time, people know very little about it, and that is dangerous. For instance, since 2013 the political climate in Brazil has triggered an important number of mobilizations and demonstrations by means of social networks. However, with new developments it is clear that those spaces were and continue to be dangerous for activists and people who voice their opinions. It was not until 2018 that people started to realize that it's not possible to say whatever you want on those platforms. That debate started in 2014, but it only became popular later on; at the time it was a debate inside a bubble, for a group. And there is an important statistic to keep in mind when we are talking about Brazil: 50 percent of the population does not have internet access. That is a huge issue. On top of that, the 50 percent with access to the internet does not necessarily access it through a computer, but through mobile devices.

6. Why is it important, particularly in the so-called digital age, to establish and promote connections between Afrodescendant communities and between these communities and ones on the African continent?

In the first place, diaspora as concept means movement; the diaspora is in constant flux. For instance, in the Brazilian context, where more than 50 percent of the population is Black, when you watch a TV show you only get to see white actors. So you can think "Oh! Brazil is a white country." This means that my country was built on racist structures, on what could be called structural racism. But there is racism not only toward Blacks, but also toward Indigenous peoples who were constantly mixing with Blacks and other populations. So, first of all, I think that getting connected to Africa is essential for our population to understand where they came from. Second, for our population to understand what the innovations produced in Africa are, because for me, countries such as Kenya, Nigeria, and South Africa are great labs of innovation. They take that innovation to the USA. In the case of Brazil, I do not understand why people have a negative attitude about being Black. The only examples that remain are those of Blacks as enslaved people; Blacks are seen as worse, intellectually speaking. So, I think that establishing concrete connections with Africa could be fundamental for establishing new standards and understanding that there are other forms of being Black.

7. Who is in charge of the programming, designing, hosting, and technical support for your project?

I am the coordinator of our project. However, as our initiative is educational, centered around data collection and making visible the role of Black women in technology, we have several partners. We have people such as Carolina da Hora, who is a collaborator working with Black people on computer science; all the women from Olabi participate in PretaLab; the people from Marianita Casagrande, etc.

With regard to servers, unfortunately we need to use traditional servers, most of which are in the USA. However, here in Brazil we have a project with MariaLab in which they are building more feminist servers [*servidoras*],[3] and it will be a space to share everything that people make. It is undeniable that using servers in other countries means that any project stored on them has to abide by the laws of the jurisdiction where the servers are located. Nowadays, people use more popular services such as GoDaddy for practical reasons, but we expect to change that in the near future when we use *servidoras*, rather than *servidores*.

8. What kind of infrastructure do you use to develop your project, considering that infrastructure can include not only computers but also anything else that helps the project along?

In our project we basically use people as infrastructure. I think that collaboration and working as a team is fundamental. Also, we have a physical space here in Rio, but our main infrastructure is based on the interaction between people, and people with technology.

9. Afro-digital connections suggests an expansive terrain of possibilities that perhaps could not be achieved otherwise. What are some of the challenges in establishing such digital connections (whatever this may mean), and what could these connections create, renew, or reinforce?

I think that one of the benefits of having technology is that you can create a point of reference, or standard, and a point of departure to create connections. Digital as a term is usually connected to a white perspective; it does not seem to have anything to do with other races. However, when you use the term "Afro-digital" there is an automatic shift of perspective regarding what digital technology means. That term opens the door to a space in which digital technology is discussed as not belonging only to white and heterosexual people, who are usually inhabitants of the North. So Afro-digital to me seems something more familiar, and that makes me feel represented. I feel this is a more appealing concept.

10. Digital humanities is a current concept widely discussed in some geographical and epistemological locations. What elements of your projects do you see as contributing to a global digital humanities landscape?

Oh God, I have not heard about it. I need to do a bit more research. I am also an academic, but I did not know about this term.

11. What is the role of PretaLab in creating knowledge and in helping us to re-think knowledge creation and dissemination?

I think the first thing we need to do is decentralize what we call knowledge. Because when people speak about knowledge they usually point at particular types of knowledge that fit inside particular boxes. In that sense, I think our project serves two main objectives: first, to open up the box and bring that knowledge to other people who have never experienced it; and second, to recognize other types of knowledge that are outside of those boxes; types of knowledge that are not considered academic in a strict sense, such as peripheral practices or traditional processes carried out by people in the periphery, in the favela, in the shantytown, etc. For instance, in the favelas there is something called *gambiarra*,[4] and sometimes the term is used in a negative way. In addition, people think that the disputes surrounding criticisms of the term are related to language. So for instance, people here speak about the Brazilian way to do things, meaning that things are done in a bad way. But for me technology is actually inside that maker universe, which is a universe where things are made to solve real problems. And it is there where you can solve particular issues with diverse techniques or methodologies: electronics, 3D printing, programming, woodworking, biohacking, etc.; thousands of things to solve problems. I think that technology serves, and can continue to serve, as a means to transform societies. Today, however, people see technology all around the world, but there is also more inequality. Technology has not helped solve the problems of inequality—on the contrary, inequality has skyrocketed. So if technology is supposed to help people, and people are using technology more than ever before but technology is not helping those people achieve better living standards and social equality, I think there is something broken. What I think is not working properly is the fact that technology is centralized in particular spaces and particular populations. And today when people speak about technologies, particularly digital technologies, they are speaking about power and decision-making processes, because it is through those technologies that really important decisions are made in our current world.

12. What is your project's target audience?

PretaLab is primarily designed for Black women. However, it is addressed to any person who is not part of that privileged group with constant access to technology. In that sense, we would like to connect with people from the periphery, trans and LGBTQ people, etc. But as I mentioned at the beginning of the interview, it is meant for Black women because I think: Who is going to change this world? Because people in general are thinking that it is the traditional groups of white men who are going to solve the problems of the world. Last year I spoke at several venues about our projects; however, I think that people did not associate the work that I presented with the questions of citizenship and human rights that are very important in our work. Because in speaking about technology you are really talking about human rights and citizenship.

13. With respect to human rights, what is the idea of the human that is at the core of your projects?

Several decades ago in Brazil, Black people were not considered human. They were seen as a workforce, as machines executing labor, they were objectified. So I think that the conception of human in our projects is something basic geared toward teaching the general public that Black folks are people who have rights, who think, who produce and not just consume. But even more important, those human beings are also producing critical work to think about their own time, their own world. I think that nowadays in Brazil people have a strong generation made up of Black people who came from the periphery and were able to attend college, all of them sponsored by the most recent democratic governments. Today, however, people do not know exactly what is going to happen.[5] Nonetheless, this generation is able to show through both practical and theoretical actions that they are humans, that they can contribute to society as much as any white person. So I think it is a quite basic issue when we speak about people's humanity because people are constantly proving they can reinvent themselves over and over. For instance, the people who work in our projects do research despite the fact that most of them have not been formed as researchers, and their research is used to claim their rights.

14. What would be the role of digital tools in making racism visible and overcoming it?

A short time ago, I thought that digital tools were central to making racism visible because, beginning in 2011, several projects and activities centered around digital tools started to appear, and that allowed Black Brazilian people to become visible. And that is very important, because people in general are seeing the existence of issues and communities that were kept in the shadows and were presented as inexistent here in Brazil. In that sense, digital tools were fundamental in order to make visible something that was presented as invisible. That is my history with digital tools: I am able to make my work—my craft—visible thanks to these tools and the way they are being used nowadays.

On the other hand, although Black people understand the benefits of these tools and take advantage of them, they remain very vulnerable because these tools are a source of power and are connected to power, to world elites, and to privileged groups in the world; not only in Brazil, but in the entire world. That is why we currently have a more careful relationship with such tools because they are not Disney-type objects or playthings. It is becoming serious; very serious and dangerous.

15. What other digital projects and initiatives are you currently working on or planning to work on?

All the projects that I have worked on and that I plan to do are related to the area of training and education. I am quite interested in the decentralization of knowledge. In that sense, our people are going to start a computer science course but with methodologies that connect people. When you speak about technology, most of the people around here do not understand what you are referring to, or they think that it is very distant, or a reality far away from their own lives. So we are having people enroll in a course—a new course that will start soon—based on the idea of creating methodologies to make content and technologies more accessible to ordinary citizens and to Black women in particular. I think that my mission is to create interest in our communities so they can engage with those themes. Technology is usually presented in a very technical and distant language that discourages "normal" people from getting involved.

The way we manage to attract people is by using knowledge they already have and can merge with new knowledge. For instance, and as I mentioned before, sewing practices, knitting, and other types of crafts already used and developed by our audiences are connected to programming and 3D printing.

16. What is the relationship between Paulo Freire's *Pedagogy of the Oppressed* and your digital projects and initiatives?

Actually, I prefer to think about *Pedagogia da autonomia* [translated as Pedagogy of Freedom], another of Freire's works. However, maker culture as a whole—although that term is very centered in North America/USA—is an example of a pedagogy of autonomy. I think that the impact it has on people is that it makes them realize they can do all those digital things with which they are presented. In that sense, if the oppressed can speak, they can say "Oh, great, I can do this and that; I am also able to understand it." And that for me is the great achievement of the maker culture as a culture of experimentation; a culture where mistakes are fairly common and you do not need to be right all the time. Because if you are poor and Black, our tradition has taught us that you cannot make mistakes. If you have an opportunity, you have to grab that opportunity and excel by being the best. And with regard to maker culture: here in Brazil we are currently speaking about a pedagogy of autonomy. When you are able to program your own website, it amazes you. That was what happened to me.

Notes

1. https://www.pretalab.com/.

2. https://datalabe.org/.

3. The Portuguese word for "servers" (*servidores*) is masculine, which Silvana converts to feminine (*servidoras*) in order to emphasize PretaLab's mission to combat gender discrimination in the Brazilian tech industry.

4. The term can be roughly translated as "quick fix." However, its actual meaning is connected to the idea of inventiveness or the ability to make something out of nothing.

5. This conversation was carried out in 2018 when Brazil was transitioning from the governments of Luiz Inácio Lula da Silva, Dilma Rousseff, and Michel Temer to Jair Bolsonaro's far-right politics. Bahia's expression of uncertainty allows us to understand the fear and insecurity activists, scholars, and people from other sectors were feeling and continue to feel with such change.

3

Afro-Latina Minimal Computing

Interview with Sandra Abd'Allah-Álvarez Ramírez

EDUARD ARRIAGA AND ANDRÉS VILLAR
TRANSLATED BY EDUARD ARRIAGA AND ANDRÉS VILLAR

Sandra Abd'Allah-Álvarez Ramírez—also known as Sandra Álvarez Ramírez—
is an Afro-Cuban activist whose blog *Negra cubana tenía que ser* has played
an important role in calling attention to issues of race and gender in Cuba.
Abd'Allah-Álvarez Ramírez is also a co-founder of the group Afrocubanas and
the designer of *Directorio de Afrocubanas*, an online project that features the
work of Afro-Cuban women in diverse fields. Abd'Allah-Álvarez Ramírez has
published extensively online and in print and maintains an active presentation
schedule. In 2014 she was nominated for the Deutsche Welle Best of the Blogs
award. Abd'Allah-Álvarez Ramírez currently resides in Hanover, Germany.

*   *   *

1. Where do digital tools fit into your media toolbox (in contrast to analog
or more traditional media)?

Well to tell you the truth, I don't know what such analog tools would be. I
have been using digital tools for many years now, ever since I graduated from
the Faculty of Psychology. At that moment I was a neuroscientist pursuing
research about the brain, and I was always accompanied by a computer, by
software—and I could say that it was then that my interest in the digital was

born. After this, my life veered toward digital journalism while working with a publisher for eleven years, and during those eleven years I established my blog and learned the most important features for updating and maintaining websites. I created websites and edited them—I was also working as a web editor—and that is how I came into contact with the digital environment.

2. What attributes or characteristics of digital tools are the most useful for you and your practice?

For me, the most useful characteristics are flexibility, the possibilities for learning, of being self-taught, of learning by doing, of arriving via different routes to the same goal; the digital has all of this, and it's this flexibility that lets me make use of it. This—flexibility—is the fundamental characteristic that I see in the digital.

3. What are the positive and/or negative effects of the digital on your culture (national, regional, ethnic)?

As to positive and negative effects: in my culture—I don't know if this is the answer you are looking for—I think that in my culture the digital is present universally. For example, my cellphone broke recently and I attempted, or rather thought about or had the urge, to not have a cellphone anymore, but it's impossible to go back to a landline. The digital, the immediate, the language of ones and zeros, is more present overall in our lives, and so one cannot escape it. For example, my grandson is three years old and takes pictures with a cellphone, and looks for his games and plays them on it. He does everything with the cellphone. He is only three and has had it since he was one and a half. That is, the digital is almost like something innate, something that can no longer be put into question.

4. How does the digital help to connect, or re-connect, the African continent with the diasporas? Why do you think establishing or maintaining such connections is important in the so-called digital age? What role do the nostalgic and the utopian play in these kinds of projects?

Well, in that sense, the social networks within the digital—especially the social networks—have played a very important role. But when the social networks weren't around, it was the forums, it was the conversation groups, it was the chat, it was other things. When I started they were not called social networks, they were called different things. And yes, they permit many people to connect; and many people are able to interact, whether one of them is in Sri Lanka and the other one in Cuba. It's too bad that in Cuba, connectivity is not enough for people to pursue activism or communicate and form communities, and so on and so forth. Communication in Cuba today, and making use of the digital, is mostly for immediate uses—for example, to communicate with relatives to resolve daily problems, and not to develop as a community.

With respect to Afro-diasporic communities, it's the possibility of interacting and seeing that other people have the same necessities, the same experiences. I am currently in several groups of Afro women: Afro-Colombian, Afro-diasporic—however we want to call them. And yes, it's very interesting to see how one can interact with people who are very far away and who have the same life experiences one has.

I am very present on social networks, on my blog, and on my *Directorio de Afrocubanas* [Directory of Afro-Cuban Women].[1] For example, people who ask me: "Are you the Black Cuban, the one with the blog?" Or when I was in the United States and had the possibility of knowing several people who basically follow me on Facebook. One of them even had a presentation at UMass, the University of Massachusetts; a person with whom I read, and so on, and who asked me: "Aren't you coming to your presentation?" And what happened was that this person was organizing the presentation. She was waiting in the room for me to arrive to present me and to deal with all the technical things. It's very interesting how the digital seems to shrink space and connect us much more.

5. Why is it important, particularly in the so-called digital age, to establish and promote connections between Afrodescendant communities and between these communities and ones on the African continent?

Of course it's very important, about Africa; the image of Africa is that of misery, of hunger, of health problems. And it's not like that, or rather many other places are like that, not just Africa, but that's what the media sells us. Therefore, it's important to be connected. It's a pity that in Cuba we have the language barrier, and me specifically, because it taxes me, much more since I have been living in Germany. It's very difficult for me to communicate fluently in English, and it's a pity because there are so many important figures in all facets of African life and culture. There is so much to know about Africa that doesn't conform to that placard of a child with a sad face, totally malnourished and looking toward the horizon. There is much to learn and much to know, and the social networks help us a lot with that. I, in particular, participate in *Global Voices* [an online multilingual community of writers, bloggers, and digital activists that aggregates and translates news produced by citizen journalists across the globe], where there are translated texts by many people from Africa, Asia—from the five continents. It's very interesting, and all this is because of the digital environment.

6. What is the role of the nostalgic or utopian in digital projects designed to re-connect or make visible Afrodescendant cultural components? What is the role of those values in your *Negra cubana* project?

About the role of the nostalgic or utopian, well it would depend on how you defined what constitutes nostalgia and utopia. But if I understand what you are getting at, for me both things are connected to Cuba; to my life experiences as a Cuban woman born in 1973, in the midst of a socialist revolution, and with the reality that now, and for the last four years, I have been a woman who has emigrated. And this second condition of being a woman who moved away has made me cast my gaze toward the issue of migration and the issue of people who are refugees. In my blog I have a small section about migrant women. And also, given my own condition, one day I had the idea of launching a newspaper for Spanish-speaking people in the city of Hanover in northern Germany where I live. I have a column in it entitled "Una cubana en Alemania"[2] in which I laugh at or problematize my day-to-day experience here as a thirty-something- or forty-something-year-old woman living in Germany.

7. Who programs, designs, hosts, and provides technical support for your project? Are these various actors local, or are they connected to more widespread, even global, servers and services? What impact do you think this has, if any, on the nature of digital projects such as yours?

I, Sandra Álvarez Ramírez, am in charge of the *Negra cubana*. Two people also help me: with the *Directorio de Afrocubanas*, the Chilean feminist Alejandra Aravena; and with *Negra cubana*, mostly Gedel, a Cuban friend who lives in the Czech republic. But basically, I do absolutely everything: the editing, the layout, the web editing; everything that has to do with web maintenance, with the plugins, with everything. And it's a challenge because I have to keep on learning; I can't let myself age in the digital environment. I have to keep on studying, and that takes time. When it's something that's beyond me because it has to do with programming languages, I look for one of those people. When I was in Cuba, however, I worked in *Cuba literaria* editing web sites and I edited in html. At that time Dreamweaver was the software to use, and so html and other such stuff, that I can do. Something that's a bit more complicated, more complex—that I pass on to acquaintances, people who support me with much love and dedication. You ask me to think about infrastructure beyond the computer, but that's basically what I use; nothing more. A domain and a server, both of which are paid for. That's it and nothing else.

8. What benefits and/or drawbacks do you see in the term "Afro-Digital," particularly if you reflect on your own practice?

This is really the first time I encounter the term "Afro-digital" or the Afro-digital world. I've participated in a few "digital" activities directed mainly toward Afrodescendant populations, but I have never participated in anything that I can say has its origin in that. I don't even know what the Afro-digital entails or in what contexts it's used. I really don't know, and so I don't know what to say.

9. Afro-digital connections suggests an expansive terrain of possibilities that perhaps could not be achieved otherwise. What are some of the challenges in establishing such digital connections (whatever this may mean), and what could these connections create, renew, or reinforce?

Yes, I do have those connections because they are low-budget projects. What do I mean by low-budget projects? To this very day I find it problematic to consider getting revenue from advertising; because of this, things have to be low-cost. Perhaps if I had advertising and earned something from it, my projects would be profitable and I could do other things. But my projects are simple. First, because they're directed toward Cuba, where connections are terrible and the more there is on a website or blog, the more difficult it is to load it and hence to be seen in Cuba. And second, because I seek to do more with less.

I establish all types of connections, and these are fundamentally feminist connections. For example, in 2015 I worked with the people of [the musical group] Afro-Kraut. I also developed the project *Ennegreciendo la Wikipedia*.[3] But I repeat, my connections are overwhelmingly feminist, because within the Black movement there is much machismo, much sexism.

The blog *Negra cubana* was the first blog in Cuba to deal with the topic of race. Nevertheless, to this day I have connected to maybe only three people because they are Afro. This is because, beyond the fact that they are Afro, what interests me is what they are proposing. For example, I am collaborating with *Afroféminas*, which is a project I learned about or detected its existence as soon as it came out.

I do not live in a comfort zone; that is, I could describe myself as a free electron, because I'm interested in so many topics. I'm interested in *negritudes*, in racism, but I'm also interested in everything that has to do with migrant women, with women in literature, with Afro-Cuban women, with feminism, with gender violence, and also with discrimination based on sexual orientation, on gender identity. The themes are diverse, and generally one finds spaces dedicated to one thing but not another. So for example, a person can have a digital project about homophobia, but this same person might not take into account the topics of racism or white hegemony.

10. Digital humanities is a current concept widely discussed in some geographical and epistemological locations. What elements of your projects do you see as contributing to a global digital humanities landscape?

Yes, I have heard about the digital humanities, because in Cuba I was in charge of the first digital humanities event that took place there. And we had a camp— ThatCamp[4]—with Alex Gil, an American-Dominican, in charge of it. We had university professors and researchers come to the event, primarily from Canada and the United States. So in Cuba you had this first group of people interested in the digital humanities, and I was there from the first moment. After that there was another event. But now I'm no longer in Cuba, so I'm somewhat disconnected from the digital humanities projects there. But I belong to a digital humanities organization that is international in scope.

When you ask me about my own projects, well, my blog has been up and running for eleven years now, and in its current format the directory is a year and a half old. I have to say that when I learned what the digital humanities were—it was what I had been doing for many years. I think that it's a very, very valid field of action, and that in our country, which is in a process of development, we could achieve much more if we had many more people who were interested in it.

The digital humanities as a concept is not popular or well known, perhaps because the digital humanities are premised on having particular resources that are usually found in universities and research centers. When you tell someone about the digital humanities, they appear puzzled: What are the digital humanities? What do they refer to? As far as I understand them, they constitute a novel proposal for renovating the subject by means of the digital environment and vice versa; the digital environment would "live" for the subject's benefit. This is how I understand the digital humanities, and it would be interesting to make use of it to make visible those populations that have been exempted from, or denied access to, the circuits of hierarchy and the circuits of knowledge. That could be one of the applications of the digital humanities for the benefit of people who have been pushed to the periphery, who have been marginalized. There is, somewhere, a digital encyclopedia of the Caribbean, which could be a good example of this.[5]

Cuba, as a developing country, has few resources dedicated to the digital. There are a great many actions, and many transactions that can be done in a digital environment but that are basically impossible to do in Cuba. Hopefully, the digital humanities movement can grow in Cuba because I think there is a lot of talent there, and there could be an interest in seeing how things go. The same goes for the Black communities, which in Cuba are not really communities in that they are not as closed as the concept of communities seems to indicate.

Returning to the topic of the digital humanities, I forgot to mention that the *Directorio de Afrocubanas* could be an example of what was called humanities computing. This is precisely what it would be because it's a directory about the life and work of Afro-Cuban women who have contributed but who haven't been recognized by official histories.

I wish programs and tools could be developed that, for example, could be used to analyze texts for racial prejudices and things like that. One of the things that interests me is working on racism or racist stereotypes in literature. That involves reading a great quantity of books or bibliographies, so it would be good to be able to insert a PDF into a program and say: here we find racist stereotypes of this kind, and of this kind, and of this kind. Something like that would be very interesting.

Notes

1. https://directoriodeafrocubanas.com/.
2. "A Cuban woman in Germany." Translation by the editors.
3. The translation of the website name is Blackening Wikipedia.
4. https://thatcamp.org/.
5. Sandra Abd'Allah-Álvarez Ramírez's reference is to *EnCaribe*, an online encyclopedia sponsored by the Fundación Global Democracia y Desarrollo, which is based in the Dominican Republic. http://encaribe.org/es.

4

Race, Gender, and Sexuality in Cuban Digital Culture

MAYA ANDERSON-GONZÁLEZ

Many early critics feared that internet use would lead to social isolation and a breakdown of communication between people as virtual reality gradually replaced face-to-face human interactions.[1] Today, even as we are reminded that "popular visions of new technology have tended toward technological determinism since Ancient Greece,"[2] theoretical approaches of "the digital" still oscillate between deterministic pessimism and utopian optimism. While some are convinced "the internet is killing our culture,"[3] others compare tweeting to writing haikus and herald the internet as "a massive and collaborative work of realist art."[4] However, an expanding body of research is concerned with the digital domain and thinks beyond polarized viewpoints, consistently showing that "the internet is an extension of real life."[5]

According to recent research, which has privileged ethnographic approaches to understanding digital technology and its users, the digital and analog aspects of culture appear so intertwined in users' daily lives that online interactions are considered just "another aspect of the same offline relationships."[6] Postill and Pink's[7] study of social media in political activism corroborates that the digital domain acts as an additional and complementary aspect of interest-driven, offline face-to-face interactions, even when they are used in punctual ways to reach specific, ephemeral goals. What's more, Madianou and Miller[8] found cultural variation in use of the internet and other information and communications technologies (ICT) within the specific context of transnational migrations. They observed that digital and analog media were used for different communication purposes and selected depending on their suitability for a particular interaction, which shows that digital interactions have not replaced analog communication but have instead allowed users to increasingly layer their interactions.

Approaching digital technology as embedded in specific cultural contexts has meant turning away from the utopian belief that heralded the internet as essentially neutral, free, and democratic. For scholars like Lisa Nakamura and Anna Everett, who address the issues of race, representation, and discrimination in US digital culture, the digital domain is not just an added layer of culture; it's an added layer of hegemonic white, Anglo-Saxon, Western culture. As Nakamura puts it, "The internet is . . . a postcolonial discursive practice, originating . . . from both scientific discourses of progress and the Western global capitalistic project."[9] From this standpoint, it appears more important than ever to turn our attention outside of North America and the English language–dominated Web when discussing race, gender, and sexuality as factors of access to the internet and ICT.

More than a decade after the groundbreaking edited volume *Latin American Cyberculture and Cyberliterature*[10] (2007) paved the way for looking at digital culture as the place where strategic uses of technology could respond to dominant global culture, this article sets out to highlight the pioneering role of Afrodescendant women within Cuban digital culture. In a context where the intersectional study of race, gender, and sexuality are largely missing from studies of Caribbean digital culture,[11] this article addresses how technology has shaped representations of race, gender, and sexuality in a country where internet and ICT penetration has been very gradual and subject to constant tension. In Cuba over the past decades, technology has often been caught between the demand for development and access, which is limited due to material hardships combined with protectionist government policy. Considering these facts, this article tries to steer clear of "a development paradigm, in which the global south only becomes a part of first world discussions at the point of what it lacks."[12] Its focus on Afrodescendant women users of digital technologies intends to heed Anna Everett's cautionary advice to not let "the global focus on the racial digital divide . . . obscure from view the important progress and innovations in information technologies (IT) taking place in Black communities across the globe."[13] In the case of Cuba, Afrodescendant communities use digital technology, specifically blogging, for building collective memory and for bringing identity politics to the forefront of the national agenda.

Digital Culture without the Internet

In an article published in *Wired* in the late 1990s, Patrick Symmes describes the ambivalent nature of the Cuban government's relationship with the internet: "In October 1996, the revolution connected full-time to the Net. . . . The Cuban regime issued a statement declaring access to the Internet a 'fundamental right' of the Cuban people, and the hundred-odd computer clubs around the island prepared for its arrival. Shortly after, the government quietly changed the rules, making it virtually illegal for ordinary Cubans to buy a computer."[14]

As accurate or biased as it may be, Symmes's concise description harks back to the oscillation between utopian optimism and deterministic pessimism I presented earlier as a predictable, albeit contradictory, reaction to the arrival of new technology. The arrival of such technology also had special significance in Cuba in the mid-1990s. At the time, the country was going through a severe economic crisis, which eroded many of the government's pillar education and healthcare programs.[15] All forms of discrimination flared up at this time—despite a constitutional ban on discrimination in Cuban institutions since 1976[16]—and disenchantment tore its way into the country's social fabric as the moral values many had fought for during the revolution were shaken to the core.

Given the context, the internet presented a strategic challenge for the Cuban government. On the one hand, it gave Cuba the opportunity to circumvent the US embargo that hindered Cuba's technical advancement, which resulted in "an information blockade that motivates official and unofficial uses of the internet to bypass the constraints."[17] On the other hand, it provided the outside world—and potentially Cubans living on the island   with unprecedented access to information that wasn't officially vetted. This dilemma led to the government's ultimate decision to restrict internet access to key institutions that belonged to priority sectors of the Cuban economy, like the official press media, medical institutions, and the tourist industry.[18] By the early 2000s, Cuban and foreign nationals who worked in these sectors were able to access different types of services, ranging from intranet and national and international e-mail to full internet access from their workplace or home dial-up connections.

In addition to the Cuban government's protectionist policy regarding access to and disclosure of information, very real infrastructural problems continue to make internet access technically and financially difficult in Cuba to this day. Both of these factors, among others, have contributed to making the island one of the most poorly connected countries in Latin America.[19] However, notable changes in access policy occurred in 2012, after the completion of an undersea fiber-optic cable between Cuba and Venezuela. The Cuban government announced that citizens would be allowed to purchase full internet access in accredited institutions, although the cost remained prohibitively high for most Cubans.[20] Since then, the percentage of internet uses in Cuba has been growing quickly. The latest statistics published by the International Telecommunications Union show that 57.15% of Cubans were internet users in 2018[21] (compared to 29.07% in 2014),[22] though the term "internet user" is not defined in the report. In June 2015, the installation of WIFI hotspots in city centers throughout the country was another step toward helping more Cuban citizens get online, which the private internet *World Stats* website reports as being as high as 33.6% in June 2016.[23] In January 2017, Cuba completed the first phase of a free home-connectivity-plan trial, which involved connecting two thousand homes to the internet in the historic neighborhood of Old Havana.[24] Despite the slow dial-up technology and the expensive monthly service charge that came into effect once the trial period ended in February 2017, Cuba seems to be slowly working toward breaking down the biases it created with decades of selective access policies.

Yet the digital divide in Cuba continues to be very real. First based on strategic and ideological merit, it is now rooted in purchasing power and broadly favors young urban dwellers, a situation that contrasts deeply with the government's explicit aspiration to implement a policy "oriented towards a socially-minded and intensive use of technological resources for the benefit of as many people and institutions as possible."[25] Researchers like Cristina Venegas and Milena Recio were among the first to take stock of the consequences these contradictions had on Cuban society and its digitization process. Venegas describes a situation where restricting access to an elite minority created "a new social contract"[26] between the state and certain individuals, from which many felt left out. In addition to decrying the social hierarchy created between the "haves" and the "have nots," Recio also draws attention to the lack of public consultation that affected the development of Cuba's social access policies.

However, both Venegas and Recio are careful to point out that restrictions to internet access haven't proscribed the development of a digital culture in Cuba. As Recio puts it: "Physical disconnection doesn't necessarily cause cultural disconnection."[27] Writing in the early 2000s, Venegas sensed that cultural use of the internet would determine Cuba's place in the digital domain. As she put it, "despite the limits to internet access, with their resulting social tensions, the current era in Cuba will be deeply affected by the professional, amateur, unpolished, biased, utilitarian, promotional, and oftentimes outrageous work that appears on blogs."[28]

Diversity in Cuban Digital Culture

Like many subjects in Cuba, discussions of digital culture and diversity are often first broached in political or ideological terms. When Cuban citizens residing on the island, most of whom were professional journalists, first started blogging in the early 2000s, many were concerned with offering a counterbalance to the anti-government sentiments that dominated the blogosphere up until that point.[29] Insofar as "these publications promise to 'speak of Cuba from Cuba,'"[30] the bloggers' views and voices introduced an alternative discourse to the mainstream narrative about Cuba on the Web, but they also paved the way for interpreting diversity through the rhetoric of ideological convictions shrouded in journalistic objectivity. In 2008, when the Spanish newspaper *El País* awarded the Ortega y Gasset prize in journalism to controversial Cuban blogger Yoani Sánchez, views about blogging in Cuba became polarized. As a result of Sánchez's personal political stance, the blogosphere was overwhelmingly interpreted as a place where political powers vied for ideological control both on the island and abroad, and the simple act of blogging from the island was hastily equated with political subversion.

In 2011, North American university professor Ted Henken published an academic article that reinforced a strictly ideological representation of the Cuban blogosphere. In the article, Henken set out to map the Cuban blogosphere, identifying four blogging platforms created between 2005 and 2008—*Voces Cubanas*, *La Joven Cuba*, *Havana Times*, and *Bloggers Cuba*—and classifying them according to their relationship with the Cuban government.[31] Although the article generated relevant debates about inclusion and exclusion within the Cuban blogging community,[32] the author's intentional focus on each platform's political stance thwarted any discussion about how other factors such as race, gender, or sexuality fit into the inclusion/exclusion mechanisms at play in Cuban digital culture.

Concurrently, in the early 2010s, Cuban researchers such as Sandra Abd'Allah-Álvarez Ramírez,[33] Yasmín Silvia Portales Machado,[34] Milena Recio,[35] and Elaine Díaz and Yudivián Almeida Cruz[36] published several studies that provided a more complex picture of diversity in the Cuban blogosphere. On the one hand, Díaz and Almeida Cruz's in-depth analysis of gender representation in the Cuban blogosphere showed that approximately 30% of Cuban bloggers were women. On the other hand, Portales Machado found that only 3.37% of these women bloggers openly addressed feminist issues or identified as feminist. As for Recio and Abd'Allah-Álvarez Ramírez, their respective research drew unprecedented attention to a handful of blogs committed to openly discussing issues of gender, sexuality, and sexual diversity in Cuba.

At the time of writing, no published research has yet ventured to map the Afro-Cuban blogosphere or explore representations of Afrodescendants within Cuban digital culture.[37] However, we do know the central role Cuba plays as a generator of Afro-Latin American cultural representations in both the analog and digital realms.[38] The questions almost ask themselves: What place do Afrodescendants hold in contemporary Cuban digital culture? Has digital culture changed representations of race for Cubans in Cuba and abroad? Though more research clearly needs to be done, a first glance at Cuba's digital cultural landscape indicates that self-affirming representations and voices of Afro-Cubans have made a place for themselves within Cuban digital culture thanks to the work of Afro-Cuban intellectuals and activists who have made it a point to bring the fight for better recognition and representations of their communities to the digital realm,[39] such as the late Inés María Martiatu, Esteban Morales, Alberto Abreu, Sandra Abd'Allah-Álvarez Ramírez, and Yasmín Silvia Portales Machado, among many others. A closer look at two Afro-Cuban women bloggers, Yasmín Silvia Portales Machado and Sandra Abd'Allah-Álvarez Ramírez, and their digital praxis will shed light on the pioneering presence of Afrodescendant women in Cuban digital culture.

As Afro-feminist LGBT activists, Sandra Abd'Allah-Álvarez Ramírez and Yasmín Silvia Portales Machado have both been creating greater visibility for diverse Cuban minority communities through blogging and social media since the mid-2000s. In addition to the research they pursue for their respective careers in journalism and academia outside of Cuba, they use their blogs as new and complementary sites of enunciation for theorizing and promoting diversity in Cuban digital culture. Their digital practices are informed by intersectionality, which "in its more expansive definition . . . is generally understood to look beyond the race-class-gender triad . . . to additional axes of difference including sexuality and ability."[40] Finally, by practicing intersectional digital activism, both bloggers carry on the role Afrodescendant women have historically played in Cuba as forerunners in producing self-affirming cultural representations of Afrodescendants in media.

Yasmín Silvia Portales Machado started posting on *En 2310 y 8225* in 2007. For eight years, this blog was an outlet for Portales Machado to express her complex, multifaceted identity, which she defines in these terms in her online profile: "Living in Cuba and being Queer has been my choice. My life is a delicate balance between motherhood, feminism, and critical Marxism."[41] Today, the blog remains a digital archive where an eclectic assortment of fictional and non-fictional texts coalesces to reflect the issues that drove, impassioned, or concerned Portales Machado as an individual from 2007 to 2015. Many posts have to do with her political activism in favor of LGBT rights in Cuba, but she also chronicles her personal experience with maternity, records travel notes on her visits to different countries, and posts her critical reflections on readings and cultural events, such as concerts, plays, or Havana's international book fair. In 2011, she co-founded the Arcoiris project, an independent anti-capitalist collective to campaign for the rights of LGBT Cubans. She is currently pursuing a PhD at Northwestern University, blogging at *Mi Vida Es Un Fino Equilibrio*,[42] and tweeting @Nimlothdecuba. She can also be found on *YouTube* and *Facebook*.

Sandra Abd'Allah-Álvarez Ramírez launched *Negra cubana tenía que ser* in 2006. What began as a kind of virtual alter ego for Abd'Allah-Álvarez Ramírez gradually became a digital tool for Afro-feminist and LGBT activism. Today, in addition to being a space where Afro-Cuban women can bear witness and challenge everyday discriminations, the blog also acts as a platform for Afro-Cuban LGBT advocacy and sociality. It's also a hub for Afro-Cuban diaspora communities worldwide and the birthplace of a currently independent digital archive of Afro-Cuban women: *Directorio de Afrocubanas*.[43] She now spends her time between Havana and Hanover, Germany, working as a freelance writer and journalist, actively contributing to Spanish-language online publications such as *Global Voices, El Toque, Pikara Magazine,* and *Azúcar&Kalt*. She tweets as @Negracubana and has registered profiles on *Facebook, Instagram, YouTube, Pinterest,* and *LinkedIn*.

Between 2005 and 2015 Sandra Abd'Allah-Álvarez Ramírez and Yasmín Silvia Portales Machado were actively engaged in Havana's digital culture scene. They both joined the non-partisan group *Bloggers Cuba*, which organized face-to-face events in Havana from 2008 to 2013, such as TwittHab I in July 2011 and TwittHab II in May 2013. Their posts as pioneering bloggers contain invaluable references to many independent and state-sponsored blogging platforms and communities that might otherwise easily get written out of Cuba's digital cultural history, such as *Cuba Blogs Club*,[44] *Bloggers Cuba*,[45] *Blogosfera Cuba*,[46] *Bloguea*,[47] *Reflejos*,[48] or *Observatorio Crítico*,[49] to name only a few.

As scholars of diversity within the Cuban blogosphere, both Portales Machado and Abd'Allah-Álvarez Ramírez have also made critical contributions to Cuban digital humanities, paving the way for other digital humanities academics to understand Cuban digital culture through the prism of intersectionality and social engagement. The debates featured on *Negra cubana tenía que ser* and *En 2310 y 8225* clearly show how the blogosphere itself became a place for generating, debating, and theorizing Cuban digital culture. In addition, the activist bloggers' physical presence (or noticeable absence) in face-to-face events that meet throughout the geopolitical North and South reaffirms the assertion that "social media practices cannot be defined as phenomena that take place exclusively online"[50] and brings issues of diversity to the forefront of academic work being conducted on Cuban digital culture.

For instance, both Portales Machado and Abd'Allah-Álvarez Ramírez were part of the organizing committee for the international digital humanities event ThatCamp Caribe 2, which was hosted by Casa de las Américas in Havana in November 2013.[51] They also collaborated with journalist, blogger, and university professor Elaine Díaz as she launched the Observatorio de la Blogosfera Cubana,[52] a short-lived yet ebullient project that gave public access (on *Facebook* from March to September 2013) to current academic research about the Cuban blogosphere. Finally, Portales Machado was part of the Cuban delegation that traveled to the Latin American Studies Association (LASA) in June 2013, where she presented research on the demographics of the Cuban blogosphere[53] and engaged in a highly symbolic act of solidarity by reading Sandra

Abd'Allah-Álvarez Ramírez's conference paper "Cyberfeminismo en Cuba?" since the author had been denied a visa to travel to the event.[54]

Digital Praxis and Intersectional Activism in Cuba

Creating and disseminating narratives that challenge dominant scripts within mainstream outlets is usually understood as a benefit of digital culture, and specifically of blogging. However, there is evidence that Afrodescendant women were already challenging mainstream media in Cuba as early as the nineteenth century. In 1888, despite bearing the brunt of gender and racial stereotypes in popular culture, which was dominated by white colonial masculine discourse,[55] a group of Afrodescendant women journalists and writers successfully published self-affirming representations of Afrodescendants in *Minerva: Revista quincenal dedicada a la mujer de color*, where they openly addressed topics like Cuba's African heritage, the experiences of slavery, and cultural self-improvement.[56] Though it was short-lived (1888–1889) and its board of directors was all male, many contemporary Afro-feminists consider *Minerva* as setting a precedent for Afro-feminism in Cuba insofar as it was the first mainstream print media outlet for non-white women to express themselves and address middle-class Afrodescendant women's double discrimination in Cuban society, based on both race and gender.[57]

During the first half of the twentieth century, after attempts by Afrodescendants to organize politically were brutally repressed,[58] Afro-feminist concerns were all but subsumed under the white middle-class women's fight for suffrage, and later, from the 1960s to the 1980s, were swept up by the revolutionary government's priority to integrate all Cuban women into the workforce. As the Constitution clearly states: "La mujer y el hombre gozan de iguales derechos en lo económico, político, cultural, social y familiar. El Estado garantiza que se ofrezcan a la mujer las mismas oportunidades y posibilidades que al hombre, a fin de lograr su plena participación en el desarrollo del país."[59]

It wasn't until the mid-1990s that a group of Havana-based women professionals who worked in media—many of whom were Afrodescendant—decided to form an independent association to respond to the long-standing trope in leftist Latin American culture that stigmatized feminism as "a bourgeois import from imperialist nations."[60] They formed the Magín collective, whose mission was to fight "discrimination against women, the falling percentages of women represented in political life, and the re-appearance of stereotypical attitudes and behavioural patterns with regard to women [by] raising awareness in the media of these problems and gender issues more generally, and by developing a programme of study aimed at empowering women and enhancing their capacity for advocacy." The collective was quickly met with institutional resistance and only remained officially active from 1993 to 1995, but its members never stopped fighting from within their professions to provide non-racist and non-sexist representations of Cuban women in media and culture.[61]

Since the mid-2000s, the *Afrocubanas* group is a new project led by Daisy Rubiera, and formerly led by the late Inés María Martiatu, that aims to re-inscribe Afrodescendant women in Cuban history.[62] Afro-feminist blogger Sandra Abd'Allah-Álvarez Ramírez, who is also a member of the *Afrocubanas* group, sees her blogging as picking up where the Magín collective left off: "Many *magineras* (or *magines*) are part of my life. ALL of them are my elder sisters. . . . Whoever analyzes the role of the media in gender inequality is indebted to them."[63] Therefore, when Abd'Allah-Álvarez Ramírez calls out Cuban institutions and mainstream media for perpetuating social, gender, sexual, and racial inequalities today in the "Observatorio de los medios" section of her blog, she is joining in Afrodescendant women's historical resistance to discrimination through alternative media production.

For instance, in a July 2014 post, Abd'Allah-Álvarez Ramírez spoke out against persistent racialized and racist representations of Afro-Cuban women on the Cuban Ministry of Tourism's (MINTUR) *Facebook* page.[64] This critical blog post generated a two-week-long debate about racial stereotyping in Cuban and Spanish media that featured comments by members of the Cuban diaspora, Cubans residing on the island, as well as non-Cubans. Responses featured a majority of personal opinions on the issue but also links to other media campaigns aimed at fomenting tourism in the Caribbean, showing the blog post's potential as a tool for comparative analysis. In addition, Abd'Allah-Álvarez Ramírez's thorough responses to her commentators illustrate her intellectual integrity as a blogger and her commitment to outreach and activism, which she puts into practice by getting in touch with the MINTUR's *Facebook* page community manager to push the institution to question its policy on racially biased ad campaigns. The discussion ends with a post from Abd'Allah-Álvarez Ramírez linking to a newspaper editorial on the ethics of community management.

By using their blogs as tools but also as safe spaces for Afrodescendant LGBT women, both Sandra Abd'Allah-Álvarez Ramírez and Yasmín Silvia Portales Machado succeed in bringing intersectional cyberfeminist practices to a digital setting outside the global North.[65] In 2011 Yasmín Silvia Portales Machado co-founded the Proyecto Arcoiris, an "anti-capitalist, independent LGBT collective"[66] that aimed to support and represent part of the Cuban LGBT community that did not feel adequately represented by other organizations, such as the government-sanctioned National Center for Sex Education (CENESEX). In 2012 Portales Machado and several other members of Proyecto Arcoiris made unprecedented use of ICT, including e-mail, *Facebook* invitations, phone text messages, and phone calls,[67] to plan a "Kiss-In for Diversity and Equality" (*Besada por la Diversidad y la Igualdad*) in Havana. The kiss-in was organized to celebrate Gay Pride independently from the CENESEX's yearly May 17 celebration of the International Day against Homophobia, Transphobia, and Biphobia. Fewer people attended the kiss-in than organizers hoped, which illustrates one of the pitfalls of digital communication in Cuba, caused by the restrictions to access and ideological aversions discussed above. However, the event was relayed throughout the international Cuban press online[68] and Portales Machado read a citizen's declaration that was recorded and later broadcast on her *YouTube* channel.[69] Both were crucial elements for creating a digital archive of LGBT activism in Cuba.

Both *Negra cubana tenía que ser* and *En 2310 y 8225* are digital information and activism hubs for self-identified non-heteronormative Afrodescendant women. These hubs form a string of "internetworked social movements"[70] by connecting feminists throughout the Spanish-speaking world, such as the Dominican Yuderkys Espinosa,[71] the North American Tanya Saunders,[72] and the Spaniard June Fernández.[73] Thanks to their work as bloggers and activists, Abd'Allah-Álvarez Ramírez and Portales Machado played decisive roles in developing digital advocacy within their communities and also helped put Cuba on the map in terms of Latin American and Caribbean Afro-queer activism. In so doing, they engaged in what Moya Bailey calls "digital alchemy," a term she coined to describe the ways that women of color, Black women in particular, transform everyday digital media into valuable social-justice media magic that recodes failed dominant scripts: "Digital alchemy shifts our collective attention . . . to the redefinition of representations that provide another way of viewing Black queer and trans women."[74]

Conclusion: New Ways of Thinking about Race, Gender, and Sexuality?

Between 2005 and 2015, *Negra cubana tenía que ser* and *En 2310 y 8225* provided unprecedented visibility for non-heteronormative Afrodescendant women in Cuba, who were once considered "one of the most socially marginal and invisible groups [on the island]."[75] These blogs also raised awareness about discrimination and generated new representations of Afro-Cuban women in Cuban digital culture.

However, after providing unparalleled opportunities for a public voice, blogging also came with high personal costs, such as regulation or surveillance. Both Abd'Allah-Álvarez Ramírez and Portales Machado had their blogs taken offline on separate occasions[76] and both Afro-feminist activists emigrated, becoming part of the diaspora in order to reach their personal and professional goals. Although they are no longer physically present in Cuba all year, Sandra Abd'Allah-Álvarez Ramírez and Yasmín Silvia Portales Machado's digital praxis continues to tie them to internet users on the island; it also connects them to a larger Afro-Cuban diasporic community. Abd'Allah-Álvarez Ramírez's contribution to the spring 2016 issue of the *Black Diaspora Review*,[77] which showcases the work of Afro-Cuban feminists currently residing outside of Cuba, can be interpreted as a sign that she is now a recognized member of this diaspora.

Though it may be too early to say, there is still little indication that ICT and blogging technologies have instigated widespread cultural change with respect to the intersecting place of race, gender, and sexuality in Cuban society. However, by connecting to other Afrodescendant communities throughout the Spanish-language digital realm, activist bloggers like Sandra Abd'Allah-Álvarez Ramírez and Yasmín Silvia Portales Machado have reinforced the island's key position as "a cultural node [in] the 'global' network of . . . African-descendant representations."[78]

Through activist blogging, Abd'Allah-Álvarez Ramírez and Portales Machado explored new means for self-expression and "collaborative construction,"[79] believing that "a lot can be done . . . to recuperate historical memory and to disclose elements in today's laws that consecrate our rights."[80] In this way, blogging and ICT can be seen as key players in identity politics and collective memory-building for twenty-first-century Cubans throughout the world.

Notes

1. Manuel Castells, *La Galaxia Internet*, 137.
2. Nancy Baym, *Personal Connections in the Digital Age*, 25.
3. Andrew Keen, "Does the Internet Undermine Culture?"
4. Virginia Heffernan, *Magic and Loss*, 8.
5. Castells, 139.
6. Daniel Miller et al., *How the World Changed Social Media*, viii.
7. John Postill and Sarah Pink, "Social Media Ethnography," 123–34.
8. Mirca Madianou and Daniel Miller, "Polymedia," 169–87.
9. Lisa Nakamura, *Cybertypes.*, 6.
10. Thea Pitman and Claire Taylor, eds., *Latin American Cyberculture and Cyberliterature*.
11. A recent body of work has engaged critically with the digital Caribbean and its diasporas to address the issue of intersectionality. Recent examples of such work are Bordalejo and Risam, *Intersectionality in Digital Humanities* (2019); Risam and Baker, *The Digital Black Atlantic* (forthcoming); and Tonya Haynes, "Mapping Caribbean Cyberfeminisms" (May 2016).
12. Bryne Potter, "Zones of Silence."
13. Anna Everett, *Digital Diaspora*, 185–86.
14. Patrick Symmes, "Che Is Dead."
15. The severe economic crisis caused by the Soviet Union's collapse in 1989, which lasted approximately ten years, is referred to in Cuba as "el período especial." Food and energy rationing, rapid increase in international tourism, dollarization of the economy, and intensification of emigration are just a few of the extreme measures the government took when the crisis was at its worst in the mid-1990s.
16. Silvina Testa, "Memoria de la esclavitud y debate racial."
17. Cristina Venegas, *Digital Dilemmas*, 12.
18. Karma Peiró, "Internet es la alternativa para dar una información real sobre Cuba."
19. Milena Recio Silva, "La hora de los desconectados," 2.
20. Recio Silva, 16.
21. International Telecommunications Union, "Cuba Profile," Country Profile, 2018.
22. International Telecommunications Union, "Cuba Profile," Country Profile, 2014.
23. Internet World Stats Usage and Population Statistics, "Caribbean Internet Usage."
24. Larry Press, "The Cuban Home-Connectivity Trial Ends This Week."
25. Oficina Nacional de Estadísticas (ONE), cited in Elaine Díaz Rodríguez and Firuzeh Sokooh Valle, "Internet y las TIC en Cuba: Notas para un debate sobre políticas públicas," 65. All the Spanish citations have been translated into English by the author of this article, unless it is specified otherwise.
26. Venegas, *Digital Dilemmas*, 3.
27. Recio Silva, "La hora de los desconectados," 5.
28. Venegas, 173.
29. Milena Recio Silva, "Blogs Cuba: Identidad atrincherada. Segunda parte."
30. Milena Recio Silva, "Blogs Cuba: Identidad atrincherada. Tercera parte."
31. Ted Henken, "Una cartografía de la blogósfera cubana."
32. For details about this discussion, see the following three blog posts: Ted Henken, "'Esta

será tu última vez'"; Enrique Ubieta Gómez, "El falso mapa de Ted Henken"; and Yasmín Silvia Portales Machado, "De cómo Teddy y Enriquito se pelean."

33. Sandra Abd'Allah-Álvarez Ramírez, "¿Qué dicen nuestros blogs sobre género y diversidad sexual?"

34. Yasmín Silvia Portales Machado, "Voces femeninas en la blogosfera cubana."

35. Milena Recio Silva, "Cuba 2.0: Género y diversidad en primera persona."

36. Elaine Díaz Rodríguez and Yudivián Almeida Cruz, "Igualdad de género en la 'blogosfera' cubana."

37. Abd'Allah-Álvarez Ramírez's important contribution has remained unpublished to this day. Sandra Abd'Allah-Álvarez Ramírez, "Las Mujeres Negras Cubanas."

38. Eduard A. Arriaga, Fernando Sancho Caparrini, and Juan Luis Suárez, "Modeling,"

39. Self-affirming representations and voices of Afro-Cubans can be found on a handful of websites and blogs such as: https://Afrocubanas.wordpress.com/, http://inesmartiatu.blogspot.fr/, https://Afromodernidades.wordpress.com/, http://estebanmoralesdominguez.blogspot.fr/, http://Afrocubaweb.com/, and http://directoriodeAfrocubanas.com/.

40. Roopika Risam, "Beyond the Margins."

41. http://yasminsilvia.blogspot.com/.

42. https://yasminsportales.wordpress.com/.

43. http://directoriodeAfrocubanas.com/.

44. Reinaldo Cedeño Pineda, "¿Qué es CUBA BLOGS CLUB?"

45. "Bloggers Cuba | Bloggers por Cuenta Propia."

46. http://blogosferacuba.blogspot.com/.

47. http://bloguea.cu/.

48. http://cubava.cu/.

49. https://observatoriocriticocuba.org/.

50. Postill and Pink, 3.

51. Luis Rondón Paz, "ThatCampCaribe. Crónicas. . . ."

52. "Observatorio de la Blogosfera Cubana."

53. Yasmín Silvia Portales Machado, "Perfil demográfico de la blogósfera 'hecha en Cuba.'"

54. Sandra Abd'Allah-Álvarez Ramírez, "¿Ciberfeminismo en Cuba?"

55. Salvador Méndez Gómez, "Feminidades racializadas e imaginarios coloniales," 135–70.

56. Inés M. Martiatu Terry, "Escritoras Afrocubanas en el siglo XIX."

57. Maikel Colón Pichardo, "Sábanas blancas en mi balcón, negra mi condición," 43.

58. Silvio Castro Fernández, *La masacre de los independientes de color (la guerra de 1912 en Cuba).*

59. This passage is translated as: Men and women enjoy equal economic, political, cultural, social, and family rights. The State guarantees that women are offered the same opportunities and possibilities that men have, with the aim of achieving their full participation in the country's development. *Cuban Constitution* 2002, chapter VI, article 44.

60. Sonia E. Alvarez et al., "Encountering Latin American and Caribbean Feminisms," 543.

61. To name only a few, Daisy Rubiera, Inés María Martiatu, Georgina Herrera, and Norma Guillard have all been recognized internationally for their published work.

62. Sandra Abd'Allah-Álvarez Ramírez, "Las Afrocubanas ya tienen su libro."

63. Sandra Abd'Allah-Álvarez Ramírez, "Habla MAGIN."

64. Sandra Abd'Allah-Álvarez Ramírez, "Observatorio de medios."

65. Jessie Daniels, "Rethinking Cyberfeminism(s)," 109.

66. https://proyectoarcoiris.wordpress.com/.

67. Yasmín Silvia Portales Machado, "Lo que les quita el aire."

68. Sandra Abd'Allah-Álvarez Ramírez, "'Proyecto Arcoiris.'"

69. Yasmín Silvia Portales Machado, *Declaración durante Besada*.

70. Susie Jacobs cited in Daniels, "Rethinking Cyberfeminism(s)," 108.

71. Sandra Abd'Allah-Álvarez Ramírez, "Negra-lesbiana-feminista."

72. Sandra Abd'Allah-Álvarez Ramírez, "Convocatoria: Afrodescendientes en una Cuba desbloqueada."

73. June Fernández, "Cuerpos de feministas cubanas."

74. Moya Bailey, "#transform(ing)DH Writing and Research."

75. Tanya L. Saunders, "Grupo OREMI," 169.

76. See Sandra Abd'Allah-Álvarez Ramírez, "An LGBT Blog Is Suspended" and Abd'Allah-Álvarez Ramírez, "Negracubana en Cubava."

77. Abd'Allah-Álvarez Ramírez "Some Questions," 7–11.

78. Arriaga, Sancho Caparrini, and Suárez, "Modeling."

79. For a definition of collaborative construction, see Mark Sample, "Building and Sharing."

80. Dmitri Prieto, "Yasmín, una multifacética activista."

Bibliography

Abd'Allah-Álvarez Ramírez, Sandra. "¿Ciberfeminismo en Cuba? Mi ponencia para LASA 2013." Blog. *Negra cubana tenía que ser*, May 13, 2013. https://negracubanateniaqueser.com/2013/05/13/ciberfeminismo-en-cuba-mi-ponencia-para-lasa-2013/.

———. "Convocatoria: Afrodescendientes en una Cuba desbloqueada." Blog. *Negra cubana tenía que ser*, March 21, 2015. https://negracubanateniaqueser.com/2015/03/21/convocatoria-afrodescendientes-en-una-cuba-desbloqueada/.

———. "Habla MAGIN." Blog. *Negra cubana tenía que ser*, March 7, 2012. https://negracubanateniaqueser.com/2012/03/07/1442/.

———. "Las Afrocubanas ya tienen su libro: Entrevista con Daysi Rubiera e Inés M. Martiatu." Blog. *Negra cubana tenía que ser*, March 5, 2012. https://negracubanateniaqueser.com/debates/afrocubanasellibro/las-afrocubanas-ya-tienen-su-libro-entrevista-con-daysi-rubiera-e-ines-m-martiatu/.

———. "Las Mujeres Negras Cubanas: Identidad, Estereotipos Raciales y Representación en los Medios." Conference paper presented at the international colloquium "A Mulher em Debate: Passado e Presente," Funchal, Portugal, June 2012.

———. "An LGBT Blog Is Suspended Over Mention of Cuba's 1960s-Era Labor Camps." *Global Voices Advocacy*, February 12, 2016. https://advox.globalvoices.org/2016/02/12/an-lgbt-blog-is-suspended-over-mention-of-cubas-1960s-era-labor-camps/.

———. "Negracubana en Cubava, duró menos que un merengue. . . ." Blog. *Negra cubana tenía que ser*, February 22, 2014. https://negracubanateniaqueser.com/2014/02/22/negracubana-en-cubava-duro-menos-que-un-merengue/.

———. "Negra-lesbiana-feminista: Revisitando a Yuderkys Espinosa." Blog. *Negra cubana tenía que ser*, May 29, 2014. https://negracubanateniaqueser.com/2014/05/29/negra-lesbiana-feminista-revisitando-a-yuderkys-espinosa/.

———. "Observatorio de medios: Una Cuba exótica para turistas blancos." Blog. *Negra cubana tenía que ser*, July 15, 2014. https://negracubanateniaqueser.com/2014/07/15/observatorio-de-medios-una-cuba-exotica-para-turistas-blancos/.

———. "'Proyecto Arcoiris' Advocates for Coloring Cuba with the Rainbow of the LGBT Community." *Global Voices*, December 3, 2013. https://globalvoices.org/2013/12/03/proyecto-arcoiris-advocates-for-coloring-cuba-with-the-rainbow-of-the-lgbt-community/.

———. "¿Qué dicen nuestros blogs sobre género y diversidad sexual?" Blog. *Negra cubana tenía que ser*, February 15, 2011. https://negracubanateniaqueser.com/2011/02/15/%c2%bfque-dicen-nuestros-blogs-sobre-genero-y-diversidad-sexual/#more-242.

———. "Some Questions about a Post-Blockade Cuba." *Black Diaspora Review* 5, no. 2 (2015) [Published in February 2016]: 7–11. https://scholarworks.iu.edu/journals/index.php/bdr/index.

Alvarez, Sonia E., Elisabeth Jay Friedman, Ericka Beckman, Maylei Blackwell, Norma Stoltz Chinchilla, Nathalie Lebon, Marysa Navarro, and Marcela Ríos Tobar. "Encountering Latin American and Caribbean Feminisms." *Signs: Journal of Women in Culture and Society* 28, no. 2 (January 2003): 537–79.

Arriaga, Eduard A., Fernando Sancho Caparrini, and Juan Luis Suárez. "Modeling Afro-Latin American Artistic Representations in Topic Maps: Cuba's Prominence in Latin American Discourse." *Digital Humanities Quarterly* 7, no. 1 (2013). http://www.digitalhumanities.org/dhq/vol/7/1/000145/000145.html#.

Bailey, Moya. "#transform(ing)DH Writing and Research: An Autoethnography of Digital Humanities and Feminist Ethics." *Digital Humanities Quarterly* 9, no. 2 (2015). http://www.digitalhumanities.org/dhq/vol/9/2/000209/000209.html.

Baym, Nancy. *Personal Connections in the Digital Age*. Cambridge: Polity Press, 2010.

Best, Curwen. *The Politics of Caribbean Cyberculture*. New York: Palgrave Macmillan, 2008.

"Bloggers Cuba | Bloggers por Cuenta Propia." Blog. *Bloggers Cuba*. Accessed on February 23, 2017. https://bloggerscuba.wordpress.com/.

Bordalejo, Barbara, and Roopika Risam, eds. *Intersectionality in Digital Humanities*. Leeds, UK: ARC Humanities Press, 2019.

Bryne Potter, Amelia. "Zones of Silence: A Framework beyond the Digital Divide." *First Monday* 11, no. 5 (May 2006). http://www.firstmonday.org/ojs/index.php/fm/article/view/1327.

Castells, Manuel. *La Galaxia Internet*. Barcelona: Plaza y Janes, 2001.

Castro Fernández, Silvio. *La masacre de los independientes de color (la guerra de 1912 en Cuba)*. Havana: Editorial Ciencias Sociales, 2002.

Cedeño Pineda, Reinaldo. "¿Qué es CUBA BLOGS CLUB?" Blog. *La Isla y la Espina*, September 22, 2008. http://laislaylaespina.blogspot.com/2008/09/qu-es-cuba-blogs-club.html.

Colón Pichardo, Maikel. "Sábanas blancas en mi balcón, negra mi condición: Hacia una (re) evaluación de narrativas cubanas decimonónicas sobre género, 'raza' y nación en las páginas de Minerva." *Mitologías hoy* 13 (June 2016): 39–56.

Cuban Constitution of 2002, chapter VI, article 44.

Daniels, Jessie. "Rethinking Cyberfeminism(s): Race, Gender, and Embodiment." *Women's Studies Quarterly* 37, nos. 1 and 2 (Spring/Summer 2009): 101–24.

Davies, Catherine. "National Feminism in Cuba: The Elaboration of a Counter-Discourse, 1900–1935." *Modern Language Review* 91, no. 1 (January 1996): 107–23.

Díaz Rodríguez, Elaine, and Yudivián Almeida Cruz. "Igualdad de género en la 'blogosfera' cubana." *TELOS—Revista de Pensamiento sobre Comunicación, Tecnología y Sociedad*, no. 92 (September 2012). https://telos.fundaciontelefonica.com/seccion=1268&idioma=es_ES&id=2012071612050003&activo=6.do.

Díaz Rodríguez, Elaine, and Firuzeh Sokooh Valle. "Internet y las TIC en Cuba: Notas para un debate sobre políticas públicas." *Temas*, no. 74 (June 2013): 62–67.

Everett, Anna. *Digital Diaspora: A Race for Cyberspace*. Albany: SUNY Press, 2009.

Fernández, June. "Cuerpos de feministas cubanas: Yasmín S. Portales Machado." Blog. *Mari Kazetari*, March 5, 2012. http://gentedigital.es/comunidad/june/2012/03/05/cuerpos-de-feministas-cubanas-yasmin-s-portales-machado/.

Haynes, Tonya. "Mapping Caribbean Cyberfeminisms." *Sx archipelago* (May 2016). http://smallaxe.net/sxarchipelagos/issue01/haynes-mapping.html.

Heffernan, Virginia. *Magic and Loss: The Internet as Art*. New York: Simon & Schuster, 2016.

Henken, Ted. "'Esta será tu última vez'—Memorias de la última conversación que tuve en Cuba." Blog. *El Yuma*, April 5, 2011. http://elyuma.blogspot.fr/2011/05/esta-sera-tu-ultima-vez-memorias-de-la.html.

———. "Una cartografía de la blogósfera cubana. Entre 'oficialistas' y 'mercenarios.'" *Nueva Sociedad*, no. 235 (October 2011). www.nuso.org.

International Telecommunication Union. ICT-Eye ITU Data Portal, Individuals Using the Internet, "Cuba," 2018. https://www.itu.int/net4/ITU-D/icteye/#/topics/2001.

———. "Cuba" query, 2014. https://www.itu.int/net4/ITU-D/icteye/#/query.

Internet World Stats Usage and Population Statistics. "Caribbean Internet Usage, Telecommunications and Population Statistics." Accessed on February 26, 2017. http://www.internetworldstats.com/stats11.htm.

Keen, Andrew. "Does the Internet Undermine Culture?" Interview by John Ydstie. *Weekend Edition Saturday*, NPR, June 16, 2007. Audio, 5:22. http://www.npr.org/templates/story/story.php?storyId=11131872.

Madianou, Mirca, and Daniel Miller. "Polymedia: Towards a New Theory of Digital Media in Interpersonal Communication." *International Journal of Cultural Studies* 16, no. 2 (2012): 169–87.

Martiatu Terry, Inés M. "Escritoras afrocubanas en el siglo XIX. Antecedentes del feminismo negro en Cuba." In *¿Y las negras qué? Pensando el afrofeminismo en Cuba*, unpublished manuscript. Accessed on October 5, 2017. https://negracubanateniaqueser.com/2015/01/07/escritoras-afrocubanas-en-el-siglo-xix-antecedentes-del-feminismo-negro-en-cuba/.

Méndez Gómez, Salvador. "Feminidades racializadas e imaginarios coloniales en el humor gráfico de Cuba en el s. XIX." *IC–Revista Científica de Información y Comunicación* no. 12 (2015): 135–70.

Miller, Daniel. *Tales from Facebook*. Cambridge, UK: Polity Press, 2011.

Miller, Daniel, Elisabetta Costa, Nell Haynes, Tom McDonald, Razvan Nicolescu, Jolynna Sinanan, Juliano Spyer, Shriram Venkatraman, and Xinyuan Wang. *How the World Changed Social Media*. Why We Post. London: UCL Press, 2016.

Miller, Daniel, and Jolynna Sinanan. *Webcam*. Cambridge, UK: Polity, 2014.

Molyneux, Maxine. "State, Gender and Institutional Change in Cuba's 'Special Period': The Federación de Mujeres Cubanas." Institute of Latin American Studies Research Papers. London: University of London, 1996.

Nakamura, Lisa. *Cybertypes: Race, Ethnicity, and Identity on the Internet*. New Haven: Routledge, 2002.

"Observatorio de la Blogosfera Cubana." Accessed on March 14, 2017. https://www.facebook.com/Observatorio-de-la-Blogosfera-Cubana-115393045315950/.

Peiró, Karma. "Internet es la alternativa para dar una información real sobre Cuba: Entrevista con Milena Recio, periodista e investigadora social de la Facultad de Comunicación de la Universidad de La Habana." Blog. *Karma Peiró : Historias de una periodista digital*, March 4, 2007. http://karmapeiro.blogspot.fr/2007/03/internet-es-la-alternativa-para-dar-una.html.

Pitman, Thea, and Claire Taylor, eds. *Latin American Cyberculture and Cyberliterature*. Liverpool: Liverpool University Press, 2007.

Portales Machado, Yasmín Silvia. "De cómo Teddy y Enriquito se pelean en el ciberfango y me salpican sin yo pedirlo." Blog. *En 2310 Y 8225*, June 12, 2011. http://yasminsilvia.blogspot.com/2011/06/de-como-teddy-y-enriquito-se-pelean-en.html.

———. *Declaración durante Besada por la diversidad y la igualdad 28 junio 2012*. Filmed June 2012 in Havana, Cuba. Video, 3:23. http://www.youtube.com/watch?v=tZMQ258wIqE&feature=youtube_gdata_player.

———. "Lo que les quita el aire es que salgamos a la calle." Blog. *En 2310 Y 8225*, June 28, 2012. http://yasminsilvia.blogspot.com/2012/06/lo-que-les-quita-el-aire-es-que.html.

———. "Perfil demográfico de la blogósfera 'hecha en Cuba.' Primeros resultados de investigación." Blog. *En 2310 Y 8225*, June 5, 2013. http://yasminsilvia.blogspot.fr/2013/06/perfil-demografico-de-la-blogosfera.html.

———. "Voces femeninas en la blogosfera cubana. ¿Cambió algo más que el soporte?" *Cuba Literaria, Portal de Literatura Cubana*, May 27, 2013. http://www.cubaliteraria.cu/articulo.php?idarticulo=16009&idseccion=25.

Postill, John, and Sarah Pink. "Social Media Ethnography: The Digital Researcher in a Messy Web." *Media International Australia* 145, no. 1 (November 2012): 123–34.

Press, Larry. "The Cuban Home-Connectivity Trial Ends This Week, Rollout to Begin Next Week." Blog. *The Internet in Cuba*, January 27, 2017. http://laredcubana.blogspot.fr/2017/01/the-cuban-home-connectivity-trial-ends.html.

Prieto, Dmitri. "Yasmín, una multifacética activista y bloguera cubana." *Havana Times*, October 8, 2011. http://www.havanatimes.org/sp/?p=47882.

Recio Silva, Milena. "Blogs Cuba: Identidad atrincherada. Segunda parte." Blog. *Enlaces*, May 13, 2006. https://enlaces.wordpress.com/2006/05/13/blogs-cuba-identidad-atrincherada-segunda-parte/.

———. "Blogs Cuba: Identidad atrincherada. Tercera parte." Blog. *Enlaces*, May 14, 2006. https://enlaces.wordpress.com/2006/05/14/blogs-cuba-identidad-atrincherada-tercera-parte/.

———. "Cuba 2.0: Género y diversidad en primera persona." Blog. *Enlaces*, March 7, 2012. https://enlaces.wordpress.com/2012/03/07/cuba-2-0-genero-y-diversidad-en-primera-persona/.

———. "La hora de los desconectados. Evaluación del diseño de la política de 'acceso social' a Internet en Cuba en un contexto de cambios." In *Estudios sobre políticas públicas en América Latina y el Caribe: Ciudadanía, democracia y justicia social*, CLACSO-Asdi program research report, November 1, 2013.

Risam, Roopika. "Beyond the Margins: Intersectionality and the Digital Humanities."

Digital Humanities Quarterly 9, no. 2 (2015). http://www.digitalhumanities.org/dhq/vol/9/2/000208/000208.html.

Risam, Roopika, and Kelly Baker Josephs, eds. *The Digital Black Atlantic*. Debates in the Digital Humanities Series. Minneapolis: University of Minnesota Press, 2021.

Rondón Paz, Luis. "ThatCampCaribe. Crónicas. . . ." *ThatCamp.org*, November 6, 2013. http://caribbean2013.thatcamp.org/2013/11/06/thatcampcaribe-cronicas/.

Sample, Mark. "Building and Sharing." http://journalofdigitalhumanities.org/1–1/building-and-sharing-when-youre-supposed-to-be-teaching-by-mark-sample/.

Saunders, Tanya L. "Grupo OREMI: Black Lesbians and the Struggle for Safe Social Space in Havana." *Souls* 11, no. 2 (June 2009): 167–85.

Symmes, Patrick. "Che Is dead." *Wired*, February 1998. http://archive.wired.com/wired/archive/6.02/cuba.html.

Testa, Silvina. "Memoria de la esclavitud y debate racial: La cuestión de la 'identidad negra' en Cuba." *Nuevo Mundo Mundos Nuevos*, December 19, 2009. http://nuevomundo.revues.org/58153.

Ubieta Gómez, Enrique. "El falso mapa de Ted Henken." Blog. *La Isla Desconocida*, June 9, 2011. http://la-isla-desconocida.blogspot.com/2011/06/el-falso-mapa-de-ted-henken.html.

Venegas, Cristina. *Digital Dilemmas: The State, the Individual, and Digital Media in Cuba*. New Brunswick, NJ: Rutgers University Press, 2010.

5

Fighting Racism with Digital Weapons

Interview with Mónica Carrillo

EDUARD ARRIAGA AND ANDRÉS VILLAR

TRANSLATED BY EDUARD ARRIAGA AND ANDRÉS VILLAR

Mónica Carrillo is an Afro-Peruvian poet, musician, digital visual artist, activist, scholar, and member of the Centro de Estudios y Promoción Afroperuanos LUNDU (Center for Afro-Peruvian Studies and Advancement) (Peru) and Proyecto Afrolatin@ (USA). In this interview Carrillo describes how she and her organization use digital tools to advance anti-racist and Afro-Latinx digital practices. She also discusses diverse forms in which Afro-Latinx communities in the Americas manage to stay connected, intervene, and counter-attack racist and colonial spaces through a productive combination of digital and analog strategies.

* * *

1. Please tell us about the organization with which you are affiliated. Where it is from and to what is it dedicated?

Well, LUNDU is an organization that was born in the year 2001—almost sixteen years ago—with the objective of discussing or placing in the public agenda of Peruvian society topics that were not usually broached by the Afro-Peruvian movement, such as making the intersection between racism and sexism visible, dealing directly with issues such as sexual and reproductive rights, discussing topics such as exogenous racism and how it determined our socializing and living processes. And additionally, to begin discussions about the LGBT population within our own communities. Another central aspect was to use art both as a creative strategy and for social mobilization. These two dimensions—from my point of view the first one is feminist—were mostly inspired by the discussions that I personally saw taking place on the network of Afrodescendant institutions. Because during that moment the World Conference against Racism was taking place in Durban.[1] I was one of the co-writers of the world youth declaration in Durban, and in an official capacity I also facilitated in several of the venues; it was a process that began in 2000. So in a way, LUNDU's birth was inspired by these more global tendencies, but it was also greatly inspired by the Peruvian feminist movement, which at that moment had a very frontal agenda fighting Fujimorist[2] violence—such as forced sterilizations, right? It was born that way, as a very diverse group, and it was founded by me and a group of much younger persons. We didn't necessarily have much organizational experience, but we did have an interest in doing something different.

2. What has been the role, if any, of digital tools in the development of these interesting projects and ideas that are so connected to the concrete realities of Afrodescendant communities, particularly Afro-Peruvian ones?

I think it's been a gradual process in that technology—at least the latest technology—has obviously developed incrementally but also explosively in the past decade. So, speaking about the early 2000s, we used the internet but didn't necessarily have Facebook, and we weren't really using other digital tools. I think that during that period, the new technology, and especially the internet, was much more powerful in the Andean and Amazonian communities where we worked (we were working there because of our agenda about race). But I did see that our Afro-Peruvian communities didn't necessarily make much use of what was referred to at that moment as ICT—Information and communications technology. The Amazonian communities did take advantage of it, because, since there are many rivers in between, internet antennas were installed in the Peruvian jungle and in other countries, and this was something very powerful that also helped these particular communities advance in a different manner. However, during that same decade—from 2001 until 2011—I didn't see the Afro-Peruvian communities use the internet as a tool, except for office use or to communicate, but not by the community. In the case of Afro-

Peruvian communities, access to the internet as such has also been something more recent, perhaps only in the last five years; which is related to the use of cellphones, right? From approximately 2007 or 2008 until today there is much to say.

I think this is a prelude to another question you might ask me about how phones have not been useful tools for the community, and how we have developed apps, virtual platforms, interactive platforms so that the community can develop. A third issue to add to the two I brought up in answer to the previous question would be using technology for research and to bring forth things that we couldn't have made visible with a critical agenda. I think those are the three important dimensions.

3. You mentioned some time ago that you had developed some type of installation in relation to the Afro-Peruvian feminist struggle—a digital installation. What do you think are the most important digital tools for such projects? (For example, digital tools that are easily accessible, such as Google+, or more specialized tools.) Please also talk a bit more about apps and about technology used for research.

I think that a tool that was quite useful was the Afro-Peruvian Observatory [Observatorio Afroperuano]. I don't know if you have seen it—the one about the media. They've analyzed about 11,000 newspaper editions in seven years. The analysis in the first few years was all by hand; that is, we bought the newspapers every day, we read them, and we identified the treatment of Afro themes according to categories such as racist insults, racist adjectives, etc. There were about six or seven categories, and then we had a monthly summary [recorte] and one every six months. Later, however, there was a big transition when many of the newspapers began putting their publications online in full. Before, during the first stage, there were headlines, although many weren't posted. You had the principal news items, but one couldn't really access small sections, such as gossip-like ones—which there are, particularly in the more popular newspapers. All that material was not initially online. When they started posting it online, it made it much easier for us to identify sections, using keywords, and that made us realize that in our previous reports we had been missing much information. We were also able to cross-reference more information. Because sometimes doing it by hand has its limitations.

Something else that I have found interesting with respect to the other initial project—the Afro-Latino Observatory [Observatorio Afrolatino], which is still ongoing—is that it has begun to analyze media in Argentina, Chile, Bolivia, Peru, Ecuador, Panama, the Dominican Republic, and Colombia. Obviously, the only way to do all that is to use the internet.

It is also interesting to be able to compare and identify how certain words have different racial or racist weight depending on the context, and to understand the characteristics of each culture: what *chombo* means in Panama or *negro* in Argentina, where it is used in many different ways. The possibility of expanding the project, which was very local, into something global has been very useful. This has been possible basically because of the internet and the information that is available, and because of the search engines in the online newspapers or the media that is available. That is one thing I think has been useful.

I think another useful thing is Facebook, which has been—and continues to be—a very important element for accessing a younger population. This has been very important because, in a way, there is a big gap between the younger people and those who have been activists in the towns and the communities. The latter are generally older and do not have Facebook. I think that in some way the foundational work has been done by Afro-Peruvian organizations in general—and not just in Peru, but also in the rest of South America—by going to the communities and the towns, keeping in mind that a large number of people are semi-literate. That, then, is the important face-to-face work of contacting people. However, sometimes that process has not been very accessible or very interesting for people who are younger. That's a big gap. Therefore, the fact that younger people have access to social networks, specifically Facebook, has opened the possibility for LUNDU's message to expand and have support. Websites and blogs exist, but these can now be posted on Facebook. Another strategy for connecting everything, Twitter, Facebook, and the blog: you update one and it updates the others. I think Facebook has had, and continues to have, much power. I think that going directly to a blog is less common now and, at least in our community, young people do not go directly to a blog. They go to Facebook because the link is there, which is also dangerous because it is too much centralized power, although I feel we have used it to our advantage in our recent campaigns.

The other issue related to this is that, in general, the internet has been very useful for establishing international solidarity. For example, in the case against the news organization about the blackface[3] incident—did you hear about it? Well, it had an enormous repercussion because it was a scandalous incident. There were reports stating that it spurred the largest amount of online discussions of any racial incident in Peruvian internet history. According to the rankings, there had never been a case about a racial topic with as much internet traffic in Peru. So, that is something very powerful, but also dangerous.

4. Do you think that incident permitted different Afrodescendant communities and individuals to connect across the length of the Americas, or did it have an impact only in Peru?

I think it had a large impact regionally because it was the first case with those characteristics. There was another one which was not quite like it, but if I remember correctly, it did exhibit similar foundational issues in Bolivia. And because the portrayal was so scandalously racist, much information circulated publicly online, generating indignation and solidarity. There were also many reports in the mass media, which had a great impact on us because we had the attention of BBC, CNN, and PBS. That type of media has the effect of bringing more people in, not only because of LUNDU's activity and the press releases that it posted, but also because of the impact of the mass media, which helped reproduce the message on a large scale. That, I think, [is] how we can use digital tools strategically for our own benefit. The fact that in addition to conventional press releases the mass media can be made to reproduce the news, and to do so on their online portals, on television, or elsewhere—that is very powerful. It makes things massive [*masifica*].

Sometimes what we do is to make something valuable or use it to create value. We were on many publication covers. How much does a cover cost, if you were to pay for publicity, in the most widely sold newspaper—in Colombia, *El Tiempo*; in Peru, *El Comercio*? So if one adds up the impact of the work done, it also translates into a lot of money; I think it's also important to see it that way.

5. A fundamental idea that gives our book its title is that of Afro-digital connections, an idea that suggests interesting conceptual terrains or spaces of possibilities. What do you think are the challenges in using digital tools to establish Afro-digital connections between different groups or, more generally, among the diaspora?

First, that all the actors in this network, the producers and the receivers of information, remember that our diaspora is very diverse. The cultural codes are very specific, and on many occasions this marks the difference that makes it difficult to establish long-term connections that can mobilize more powerful processes. The Andean region as such has many cultural characteristics, not just in terms of languages but also in ways of seeing the world that are very different from those of communities in the Caribbean or the Spanish-speaking Atlantic. We also have the southern zone—what was MERCOSUR.[4] It's very powerful now—the Afro-Chileans, the Afro-Argentinians—but in that region we also have African migrants, or people descended from African migrants, who did not come from the slave trade but rather from a modern diaspora. I have heard about some differences in access to affirmative action between descendants from African slaves and those who arrived later.

There is currently a political conflict around that issue of agendas, of priorities. So, I feel that all of our productions should be very sincere and open about stating "I am doing this because I want to spread a message to the diaspora, but my expectation or my dream shouldn't be to think blindly about the unity of the diaspora movement in Latin America, about the unity of the movements." So always speak in the plural. If we think the other way, after a time we begin to generate superficial processes because we are all Afro and so we should love each other. But then there is no solid foundation—for example, we are in the decade of the Afrodescendants,[5] but there is no powerful movement working with that. Why? Because there isn't that specificity or differentiation between us.

Another important and positively powerful issue is that the aesthetic-political movements have much potential. Topics such as hair and clothing and their textures form what is a strong current of interest in people thirty and under, especially toward the younger end. I think those connections are less superficial because they speak not only of the hair itself—for example, my Afro hair or the use of dreads by someone in Colombia or Panama—but also about my conception of beauty, of the world, and of the "why." So although for many people those topics are very superficial, I feel that they are the most profound in this virtual dimension because they speak about something that you feel, that you love, that you carry with you. In contrast, questions about ideology are OK but you never end up arriving at the bottom because you're not speaking from your heart, from your own depth. You're speaking more about your commitment as an Afro. So I think that digital tools are much more powerful for this second group, and they are creating very cool movements.

6. In LUNDU, who develops the programming of digital tools and applications? Do you do it yourselves, or do you make use of programmers from outside your organization?

In response to the last question, I forgot to mention that in addition to Facebook and the LUNDU website we also have the Afro-Peruvian Census, which is also a web application. The Census was conceived with the idea of articulating not only with people in Peru but also in places where they can feel they are being counted, or they feel they are part of a movement that identifies as such, since talking about it is problematic. With respect to what you were just asking me, the technological installation with interactive technology as presented recently in Peru—basically, we contract programmers from outside for applications such as the Afro-Peruvian Census. In a first stage we did it that way for the Web, although now we try construct the webpages with sites like Square or Weebly. I feel these are very useful because they give us much more control over the information, and they help enormously in reducing costs, especially when you work with in-the-moment campaigns, such as with the media: a press release here, or someone says something racist, or whatever; one has to answer that. That is the purpose of LUNDU. In other words, one always has to be there on top of things. And in addition you have to call the programmer and find where they are and how they are. So having things that we can maintain ourselves also makes us faster and more effective.

I designed the programming of the interactive technology. I pursued a Master's in interactive programming; it was something I wanted to do because it was a way to place myself in the vanguard, personally and institutionally, of things that in Peru are still not being applied by the Afro movement. As far as I know, there aren't any such projects in the human rights movements. There are, however, some small things that they are trying to do with the Museum of Memory [Museo de la memoria] and the Art Museum, but not within the Afro-Peruvian movement or any other such activist groups.

The installation was finished and it was nice because it's part of an idea I'm working on that is an interactive museum of Afro-Latin memory, and which requires using the latest technology and programs such as MAX DSP and Arduino, which are not so new, since they've been around for a while. But it does imply using other languages. What we did was interesting: it consisted of a patch that was installed in a room with a camera where people could see themselves when they entered the room, but as they moved they could also hear testimonies from a book and some poems I had written that were a bit more metaphorical or not so direct. At the same time, it was an "in-your-shoes" concept; that is, you chose and assumed the responsibility for what you wanted or did not want to listen to. This generated an installation with a complete spatial ambience that made people feel they were entering the life of an Afro-Peruvian woman.

Technology makes sense for such things; it makes sense with respect to the conceptualization. I think that interactive technology is very powerful. It has feedback from the people who are there, from the audience, and this feedback can generate something else that, in turn, returns to the spectator and can generate some type of change—a dialogue. I think that it's there at a personal level: the personal hope I have that I can generate proposals in which I can establish a dialogue without my being there, that the person experiencing it can feel affected, and that such an experiential impact can transform some of what we are addressing.

7. In that sense, would you say you are seeking to generate knowledge by means of digital tools and the process of conceptualization?

Yes. First, to generate knowledge; second, to generate empathy; and third, to generate transformation. There are three steps. And it doesn't mean that that transformation will change them into completely different people. But since I am an artist, and in the beginning LUNDU's first events were concerts of poetry recitals, and we played [music], and that was our life for twelve years. We realized that what has made us so successful throughout these years of hardcore campaigns is that we have reached the more sensitive fibers [fibras] of the audience. This hasn't simply been a question of "let's reform the law." There's been much work leading to this, artistic work, work with the psycho-dynamic perspective of getting to people's most sensitive fibers; and to work first with what's inside, and how starting with feelings—whether good or bad—achieves a transformative process. Art is powerful because of that—you use other resources. I think that in such cases technology provides an artistic perspective, or a creative perspective, or a perspective that breaks the rules and proposes a new conceptualization of something. This new conceptualization can transform a violent person—in how this person is going to understand better the ways the legacy of slavery impacts the everyday of Afro-Peruvian women. So the only way to think in an artistic manner is seeing it as an experiential approach. The information is there, and this is where interactive technology comes in: in the dialogue permitted by this set of resources, which opens up many possibilities.

8. In that sense, what is the conception—or the conceptions—of the human that are at the core of LUNDU's or your particular projects. Or to put it another way, what type of human being are you addressing and representing by using those tools? What type of human being do you have in mind?

When you ask what type of human being, of what dimension are you speaking?

9. What humanity are you trying to form with your projects? For example, are you trying to create a more inclusive humanity by combatting racism?

OK—I understand. Well, that's an interesting philosophical question. I think there are several types of humans [and several issues that are important].

First, being able to have the space so we can express ourselves freely, and with that freedom to speak with a proper name about what we live because there are many people—in LUNDU and other places—that keep criticizing the fact that people in Peru insult you. Some have spat in my face several times because of my being Afro, when I was eleven and now when I am grown up. In other words, just saying and stating often something that is real bothers some people because they say it is a form of victimization. Even people who are Afro, who belong to the movement, say "Why speak so much about that?" But I reject that attitude, because it is something real, something that happens, and I think that, in general, technology or the projects work toward our not always having to worry about whether the aggressor is made to feel uncomfortable. That, I think, is the logic: you are the aggrieved party, but you also have to worry about not appearing as a victim—and who worries about you? So that freedom to express oneself is something powerful.

And second, it's the freedom to talk about totally different things that don't have to do with our race. That's why there are elements of LUNDU that are musical and poetical. All of the creative things we've done—projects with painting and many other things, music records we've produced—have always tried to remind us that we're not only Afro but also human beings. It's sad and hard always to be subsumed under our racial identity, without the freedom of speaking from another vantage point; to be "played" when we actually want to, and to be "played" as well when there's no other option—we lose no matter what.

So for me, freedom from the Afro point of view consists of those two issues. From the non-Afro side, it consists of assuming the responsibility of history; the responsibility of my having been placed in a privileged position with respect to Afro peoples or others; the responsibility of being able to carry some of the weight that Afro persons carry, waiting for the other person to understand either my culture or that I was brought up in a racist manner and I didn't notice.

It's important to move beyond the guilt and do something more. And speaking not as Afro or non-Afro but rather from a more metaphysical perspective, I think my personal aim or mission is to achieve a post-racialized society (in contrast, I do not see this as LUNDU's mission, because we are not living through a historical moment in which this is possible). That is, a society where these very themes of racial identity are not the ones that determine interactions with the other, but are rather simply something extra on which I can comment. It wouldn't constitute my first identity, nor to what I would dedicate my life. I feel that we're not in the political or historical moment to be able to do that. I feel that sometimes we have to be ethnocentric. I feel that we have to be radical, because only by being radical can we transform structures.

But the idea of the post-racialized society is interesting. I think that these interactive technologies permit one to think about other worlds. The title of my thesis was *The Museum of the Ancient Future* [*El museo del futuro antiguo*]; in it I try to search for a cyborg identity—no, for a cyborg spirituality. Not only in an Afro-futurist sense, but rather to think in another way. And I obviously talked about the *catacumbas*,[6] the hacienda of San José, and about slavery. But what is beyond that?

10. To which specific audiences are your digital projects directed? What audiences do you have in mind when you develop those projects?

Each project has diverse audiences. We establish a strategy or a design for political impact and for an impact on an audience. In terms of audience: well, if we want to reform a particular law, we have to convince the members of Congress and also other people. But this needs an audience-impact strategy tailored to convincing students and public figures or leaders so that the Afro-

Peruvian people can speak in their towns. In other words, we usually think in terms of segments [of the population]; there's always something global, but each product is thought out in terms of segments, which makes it powerful because in this way it reaches the sensitive fibers of the audience you want to transform, change, convince—or bother.

11. I imagine you have heard of the digital humanities. In your view, can the projects you develop be considered digital humanities projects? Would you be interested in conceiving them as such? Or do you think that your projects go beyond what the digital humanities, as an academic field, attempts to encompass?

I think the projects have a digital humanities component, although they are not conceived wholly as digital humanities projects. For example, the Afro-Peruvian Census was not conceived as a finished Afro-Peruvian Census, as a tool. It was part of a design that we named "tell me everything," "tell me about family." Many lines or approaches exist to let Afro-Peruvian people know about the Census. The digital aspect was one component, but it wasn't the central one. And I think that was on purpose. There are projects that can only be conceived as digital humanities projects, and we would like to do them. But I think we haven't been ready as a community to do something that is solely centered around a digital humanities perspective. Because in the case of Peru, the access to digital tools is something that is very recent and is still progressing.

In contrast, I saw a beautiful project when I went to a meeting at Harvard—I also saw it in Cartagena: some women from Colombia had this thing about a message that they send. It's like a map on the internet, with towns. And they go and interview people who will send a message, as they used to do on the radio: "I want to send a message to my aunt, who is . . ."—you know? It used to happen on the radio at certain times—at six in the morning, I think. Someone sent a message to somebody else in another town, and this happened on the local radio stations. For the project the women created a platform like that, where they send a message. And it's great. I think that conceived in this way it is a tool that proceeds directly from the digital humanities. That's its whole frame. In the case of Peru, I think that LUNDU decided not to make something within that frame because we felt that we weren't prepared as a community for that. At a technical level—yes, you can hire people. But I feel that only now, or perhaps in a year, will we be able to think of something with those characteristics, because the level of access people have is very recent.

12. Do you have a future project in mind?

In LUNDU we are finishing up the last project—auditing and such. We are in a kind of resting stage because it's important to take some time out to see about funding and think about new strategies. I, personally, will be publishing another book, but one about poetry. The last one I published was about ten years ago, so a lot of time has gone by. I made a record nine years ago, so I also should make another one. But the interactive museum is something that I really enjoy doing. Since I work in a museum, it's interesting to be very involved in this more artistic world—what they call here in the United States the cultural mainstream, the major museums. And to see how something can be done for the Afro-Latin community, or rather, *about*: about the diaspora. But not yet. For now, I want to rest and dance salsa for a few months because I'm very tired.

Notes

1. 2001 World Conference against Racism, Durban, South Africa, sponsored by the United Nations.

2. The reference is to the former Peruvian president Alberto Fujimori, whose terms in office (1990–1992 and 1995–2000) were characterized, in part, by a family planning policy that resulted in the sterilization of more than 300,000 people a month, the majority of whom were Indigenous women.

3. On May 8, 2018, Miguel Moreno appeared in blackface on FOX Sports Radio Peru. He was pretending to be Jefferson Farfán, a well-known Afro-Peruvian soccer player.

4. MERCOSUR is the Spanish name for the South American trade bloc established in 1991.

5. The United Nations declared the years 2015–2024 the International Decade for People of African Descent.

6. *Catacumbas*, or catacombs, are underground burial places in Lima. The places were built under the Basílica de San Francisco (Saint Francis Basilica) and got extended throughout downtown Lima. Both enslaved and free Africans were buried there as a result of the numerous deaths caused by the Black Death, brought by European travelers to Peru.

6

International Organization Theory and Online Afro-Latin America

YVONNE CAPTAIN

Introduction: International Organization Theory in a Nutshell

This chapter is a study of Afro-Latin American organizations and their engagement with the African diaspora through their presence online. The digital footprint of a group is difficult to ignore, and it is possible to learn a great deal about a community, including an organization in that community, through its internet communications. What is the extent of Afro-Latin American organizations online? Do they have characteristics in common? For the organizations whose origins predate internet usage, how does adding a digital presence make a difference in their functionality and in overall achievement of their goals? What outreach do these entities have, and how do they connect with the African diaspora? International organization (IO) theory provides one way to delve beyond the "Quiénes somos" or "Quem somos" (About us), in Spanish and Portuguese respectively, to examine such questions.

Broadly speaking, IO theory concerns itself with global governance and emerges from a broad array of disciplines such as economics, sociology, anthropology, and even the management sciences.[1] Moreover, an attuned political scientist might first consider that "international organization" in Latin America refers to entities such as the hemispheric governing body of the Organization of American States (OAS) or the regional economic force of the

Southern Common Market (MERCOSUR).[2] However, while much of the literature on IO theory does continue to focus on the nation-state as the ultimate international organization, recent scholarship opens the dialogue to include a range of non-state actors, many of which interact to varying degrees with state institutions. In fact, there is room for analysis of even the smallest of organizations that intersect beyond the community level and establish a dialogue with the state. Some such organizations manage to bypass the state altogether in order to bring their cause to a global audience via supra-national organization. This was the case with Brazilian groups at the United Nations Durban conference on racism.[3] W. Richard Scott and Gerald F. Davis's description of organizations as rational, natural, and open systems is useful here, since it encompasses entities at all these scales in a continuum from top-down control to more horizontal ad-hoc configurations. In particular, open-system organizations are more sensitive to context and, as noted in their description, open to external links and participations than the more "closed" rational and natural types.[4] Additionally, I abstracted into the table in Appendix 2 some basic parameters common to organizational analysis to use as a rough guide to an organization's effectiveness online. In this light, the organizations I look at consist of much smaller non-state actors. "Organization" in the context of this study connotes any working body that goes beyond one individual and endeavors to operate within a given society, seeking to alter at one level or another that society as it existed before the organization came into being.[5] Further, my focus is on organizations that seek ties to other African diaspora communities. I zero in on the digital diaspora in order to explore how these organizations attempt to boost their influence via online tools.

Admittedly, such a focus is heretical in the world of IO theory; yet the tools of this academic approach most fit my needs. By stripping away all but the most common denominators of meaning to define "organization" as a collective group working to achieve goals, I am able to concentrate on entities that rarely receive analysis. Although there are no claims here of theoretical contributions, it is surprising that IO theory, often on the cutting edge of scholarship, has little to say about small entities that must inevitably interact with the larger organizations central to IO. Further, there is little on the digital dimensions and effects of online contributions to the study of organizations, and the few that exist do not limit themselves to the analysis of IO.[6]

At some point, IO scholars address many of the following issues about organizations: their beginning, their mission statement, their major structural components, their membership, their audience, their decision-making process, and—importantly—their funding sources. According to Walter W. Powell, "The digital age makes substantial investments of human or financial resources in the acquisition of information obsolete, thereby rendering an organization's influence over its peers less a matter of size and resources, and more shaped by its ability to use social media and communication technologies."[7] "Substantial" is the operative word in his observation, as some type of financial backing is necessary. Further, the influence of an organization—particularly one relying on an online presence—also depends a great deal on the organization's social media skills.

The question of resources therefore elicits questions pertinent to the online endurance or survivability of Afro-Latin organizations: What tools of influence does the organization have? Why does anyone pay attention to it? This question is valid because the majority of Afro-Latin organizations decry the treatment of their communities by their governments. What makes some organizations more successful than others in gaining the attention of viewers and policymakers? When and what are the latest updates to its website or to other technologies? Communication with both constituents and the larger public is vital if an entity is to continue to receive feedback and support. What are the hot button issues on its agenda? This question also points to the animus of the moment. For example, most Afro-Brazilian organizations have vehemently protested the killing of Marielle Franco.[8] Franco's death, and similar domestic causes, dominate the pages in other Latin countries as well. What are the dialogue indicators that tie the organization to other diaspora groups? What makes this organization international in scope? If the entity does not connect in one way or another with Afrodescendants in other nations, it does not serve my research purposes, as it does not link to the broader diaspora.

This chapter is an expansion of my larger study related to Afro-Latin America and its place in the African diaspora. Here, I seek to provide specific details about organizations.[9] For this purpose, the long-standing web presence afro-cubaweb.com is a source of valuable information, but an important reference I used was *Organizaciones de la población afro-descendiente*, published by the Secretaría General Iberoamericana (SEGIB, or in English, General Secretariat for Ibero-America). I began my study before the release of the SEGIB report, although once available it gradually became an essential component to what

I write here.[10] In *Organizaciones,* SEGIB identified over eight hundred Afro-Latin organizations, established contact with nearly five hundred of these, and received upward of two hundred responses, some more detailed than other replies. One finding of SEGIB stands out: the breadth and strength of women-led organizations. Even when women choose not to belong to country-specific organizations, they gravitate toward the networks of Afro-Latin women who in turn connect with the entire diaspora. Also of note is the fact that Afro-Latin Americans themselves requested the study, which points to the current activist momentum driving Afro-Latin organizations that is paramount to all of my work on the diaspora and that is an expression of what I describe as diaspora agency. In broad terms, diaspora agency encompasses both the strategies of self-representation created by Afrodescendant individuals and communities, and the positive actions that these self-representations stimulate in the world at large. Importantly, diasporic connections, conceptual or otherwise, serve as important sources of affirmation that stimulate additional connections and increase positive actions.

Finally, some studies are beginning to examine online performance within diaspora studies but they tend to be mostly of the United States. My concern is how online connectivity affects the performance and longevity of Afro-Latin organizations. Further, I broach the need within IO theory to explore the effects of an organization's public image on the entity's well-being. Surprisingly, there are few studies of this important subject and most do not address my particular area of inquiry.

Narrowing the List: Four Key Afro-Latin Organizations

After studying more than twenty different organizations[11] as a means of approaching a semblance of representation, I focus on four differing groups that in some ways share characteristics with others of similar ilk: Educafro (Brazil); AfroAmérica XXI[12] (Colombia); *Afroféminas* (Spain); and Mundo Afro (Uruguay). When deciding which organizations and which countries to give sustained study, one initial motivation was the size of the Black community in relation to that of the country. Measurement is becoming more feasible in part because Afrodescendants in the Americas are insisting on census records that reflect their presence. Whereas prior decades saw little or no statistical data by race and ethnicity, many countries now include a self-identification category. Of all the Americas, the Dominican Republic and Haiti have greater percentages of people of African descent in their citizenry and they are worthy of a study in this regard. However, in terms of raw numbers of human beings of African descent, Portuguese-speaking Brazil has the greatest numbers of any country in the Americas, followed by Spanish-speaking Colombia. I assumed that countries with the largest populations of people who self-identify as being of African descent would also have a greater online presence to match that large population. In some cases, the results surprised me, and this reflects in the inclusion of *Afroféminas* in this study, a highly successful organization based in Spain that attracts Afrodescendant audiences from around the globe. This is an important indication of how people and organizations transgress borders in the digital age, in this case because of the transnational nature of the African diaspora.

Brazil and Educafro

Educafro was founded in 1997 by Father David Santos "to promote the inclusion of the Black population (in particular) and the poor (in general), in public and private universities with study grants, through the service of its volunteers in community centers of pre-entrance exams and the National Headquarters offices in a collective effort."[13] In its mission to help disenfranchised Brazilians, Educafro benefits from the historically significant pull of Liberation Theology, whose values and teachings are evident in the principles espoused by founder Father Santos.[14]

Among the Brazilian organizations that I reviewed, Educafro struck me as being relevant on many fronts. Its sheer organizational ability is impressive, but so is its base in Catholicism. Religion adds another dimension to the study and is an important factor among people of African descent in the country.[15] Moreover, although Educafro insists that its mission is primarily about the education of people of African descent, the organization does not exclude the poor or undereducated and recently took on the cause of immigrants.

Achieving Educafro's mission is not as simple as it appears. In a country that only recently acknowledged officially that it is not the racial democracy that it projected to the outside world, or even to itself, the work of Educafro is a herculean task. In aiming to increase the educational levels and better the social status of the nation's Black citizens and its poor, the organization uses the governmental policy of affirmative action as one means of achieving its goals. Controversial when its proponents first exercised them here in the United States, affirmative action efforts in Brazil are fraught with their own set of naysayers. In one way or another, there are cries of special privileges for undeserving multitudes. Other obstacles include removal of tacit support from government entities. NGOs—no matter how useful and successful internationally—must depend somewhat on the national governments under which they fall. As of this writing, the rightist government of Jair Bolsonaro is very different from the leftist government of Luiz Inácio Lula da Silva, and later Dilma Rousseff, under which Educafro flourished. Yet, there is some indication that Educafro will retain much of its current vibrancy and independence.

The website for Educafro is well organized and user friendly, helping to get the word out to those seeking education and funding and ensuring that as many people as possible involve themselves in the betterment of humankind. Moreover, as both part of its educational outreach and core beliefs, prominent Africans and diasporic thinkers and activists appear on their website as examples of the ties that bind people of African descent. This is in addition to the global awareness campaign that is evident in its teachings. For example, sprinkled throughout its documents one finds quotes from Martin Luther King Jr., Nelson Mandela, Pope Francis, and chapters 5 and 6 of the Gospel of Matthew in the Bible.

When the mission of an organization clearly projects its needs well into the future, and when it is capable of navigating the pitfalls of resistance, it is reasonably certain that the organization will exist for many years to come. The need for education remains an issue that will continue in the near future for large swaths of Brazilians, and with its primary focus on Afro-Brazilians, Educafro strives to meet some of that need. By expanding beyond its base in São Paulo and into Rio de Janeiro, Brasilia, Minas Gerais, and Baixada Santista, the organization is moving strategically to accomplish its goal. As long as the overall Black population of Brazil remains an underserved community, and if the Catholic Church remains a significant religious force within the country—although suffering its own self-inflicted woes—and continues to recognize the value of educating Brazil's Afro-Latin communities, it is a reasonable assumption that Educafro can survive, and indeed thrive, despite setbacks that changes in government may inflict on the country. Moreover, in terms of other support, there is a direct link on Educafro's website for donations and for in-kind contributions like volunteering one's time. These two types of "funding" serve to strengthen the organization by involving the global community. In all of these regards, Educafro provides the reader with much hope.

Colombia and AfroAmérica XXI

AfroAmérica XXI came into existence in 1995 and immediately sought to branch out strategically throughout the Americas, serving as a federation of Afro-Latin entities. Its vision states: "By the year 2021 AFROAMÉRICA will become the leader among Afro-Latin American organizations and will be recognized for its work in the areas of ethno-education, democratic development, and promotion of ethnic development. At the same time, it manages to consolidate Afrodescended civil society with the capacity for generating its own funding resources and for actively participating in the various political, academic, and social arenas throughout Ibero America."[16]

The organization's original plan showed wide support among national and regional entities, and the Inter-American Development Bank (IDB) and the Government of Canada were among the early supporters. This, along with AfroAmérica XXI's goal to become self-sustaining, was an admirable objective, with an a priori understanding that, just as governments come and go, so does support.[17] Early on, there was mention of chapters in several countries, including Argentina, Bolivia, Brazil, Colombia, Ecuador, Honduras, Mexico, Nicaragua, Panama, Peru, Venezuela, and the United States.[18] As a logical intermediate step, it chose to focus on the Andean countries and gradually radiate outward to other regions of its hemisphere. AfroAmérica XXI also sought to target generational groups, so that by 2021 younger people would benefit from its reach, particularly in the area of educational development.

The use of the future tense in a mission statement is a frequent descriptive practice, signaling in part that the organization acknowledges that it will always be in a state of becoming and of achieving its goals. This verbal tense can also signal that the entity remains at the planning stage before realizing its goals. The latter case forces me to write of AfroAmérica XXI mostly in the past tense. From the date of my initial research into the organization as part of this study, and as this book goes to press, there is little indication that the organization—as a broad networking group—is surviving its initial promise. It may be that AfroAmérica XXI morphed into other entities, as occasionally happens with fledgling organizations. However, my attempts to verify this assumption were not successful. What is evident in the table in Appendix 2 at the end of this chapter is the number of essential categories in which AfroAmérica XXI is lacking.

What went wrong? The goals and objectives of AfroAmérica XXI are laudable. Yet, vision alone does not ensure the success of any group, and it is obvious that the goals and objectives of AfroAmérica XXI did not come to fruition. Without direct communications with the founders or with those who remained with the organization at least through its 2016 last web update, no definitive answer is possible. Individual chapters like the one in Honduras post sporadic updates—for example, on the historic election of Epsy Campbell as the first Afro-Costa Rican to serve as vice president of her country.[19] However, there remains no indication that the governance of AfroAmérica XXI has shifted from Colombia to Honduras, nor is there evidence of coordination of activities. With regard to the news about the monumental election in Costa Rica, an essential question for me is, Why, in this regional network of organizations, is only one branch reporting on the monumental election in another Central American country?

From an outsider's point of view, perhaps chief among the problem areas for AfroAmérica XXI is the inability to determine leadership within the group. Even when the various organizations that comprise AfroAmérica XXI have strong leadership, someone needs to be at the helm of the supra-organization to ensure stability. Further, as of the publication of this study, the webpage lists 2016 as the date of its last revision. This is separate from the *Facebook* page of the chapter in Honduras. Many of the internal pages remain in the design phases, including with the web-hosting template visible for all to see. There is a contact page, but the contact information is not specific. There is no one person who serves as the contact liaison, rendering it difficult for communication with the leadership or any other persons involved with AfroAmérica XXI. The address does not give a clear sense of the location of the organization. Only through a reverse lookup of the phone number was I able to ascertain that as of 2016 its apparent headquarters is in Leticia in the Amazon region of Colombia, even though the organization's formation was in Washington, DC.

As mentioned above, AfroAmérica XXI began strong, with its backing from the IDB. The organization acknowledged from the beginning that this funding was not permanent or even long-term. Whether through benign neglect or financial crises of their own, regional institutions failed to pick up the slack that IDB left. Apparently, AfroAmérica XXI struggled on but ultimately ceased to operate on a regular basis. One might argue that it takes money to run an organization. Yet, as the reader can see from the example of *Afroféminas* below, that is not necessarily the case. When one manages it prudently, funding and other forms of resources can provide a huge boost to any group; but without someone in charge to ensure the smooth working of the various components of the group, it is unlikely that the organization can thrive.

Spain and Afroféminas

Spain is not a country that many contemplate when considering the presence of people of African descent today, yet in this respect it remains historically and currently important. Together with Portugal, it was one of the first sites of bondage for Africans outside of the continent at the dawn of transatlantic slavery. As a colonizer, Spain had the largest presence in Latin America, and people of African descent were among the subjects who wrenched their freedom from the colonizer. Even today, it should come as no surprise that the African diaspora is in Spain. Movement is a characteristic of all groups of people in all periods, and Afrodescendants from Latin America are no exception. Spain is significant in that people of African descent from many places reside there—continental Africans who arrived during the current great migration phase, Dominicans from the Trujillo era forward, and Latin Americans of many countries and all ethnic groups who choose this country as their new home.[20]

Afroféminas, an online magazine dating from 2014, exists within this context, and so it is an important node in an increasingly globalized Afro-Latin America. Its founder and editor-director is Antoinette Torres Soler, a woman whose vision and energy propel the organization forward. Although Torres Soler is Afro-Cuban, there are no direct linkages between the organization and her native Cuba. The expression of its purpose is succinctly evident in its name: "Afroféminas" (Afrofeminists), as it seeks to champion the plight of Black women throughout the world. It is transnational by nature, endeavoring to showcase the woman of African descent by focusing on Afrofeminism but also looking to feature youth and Afro business and culture.[21] *Afroféminas* deserves more than a passing glance because of the pattern of migration to Spain described in the previous paragraph and because it provides examples of right choices that online organizations can make. Further, it differs from many organizations in that the group is not an NGO—a fact that leaves it free to alter its activities and practices as it chooses—and in a few short years has managed to become a go-to organization for much of what is woman-oriented in the Afro-Latin world.

The first example that demonstrates its reach involves my quest for more online information about the Costa Rican poet and activist Shirley Campbell Barr (1965), which led me to *Afroféminas*, thus constituting a great example of the power of digital media. Not only does the online magazine feature Campbell Barr's works, it proudly credits her occasional editorial work there as contributing to the magazine's success. In global Black circles, Shirley Campbell Barr is already a phenomenon, and her signature poem "Rotundamente negra" (Unequivocally Black) has at least two online performances that receive a constant barrage of hits on youtube.com, regardless of which version of the poem one views and hears. Campbell's online presence, whether with *Afroféminas* and beyond, is one more example of the ability of the internet to create more level playing fields for small entities as opposed to large organizations and their bureaucratic structures.

Among many other instances that I could cite as measuring the reach of *Afroféminas*, some stem from the questions that I posed to Director Torres Soler. I wanted to know if she attended the first Summit of Black Women Leaders in 2015.[22] In our interview sequence, Torres Soler responded that while she did not take part in the first summit, she received an invitation to the second summit that occurred in 2016. As word rapidly spread about the vibrancy of the online journal, so too did requests for the organization's time. The invitation to attend the second summit and the Campbell Barr experience are but two illustrations of how quickly the organization already reaches a large segment of the African diaspora. By the third year of its existence, the *Facebook* page alone surpassed more than one million hits, and the discussions that take place on its webpage and among participants are lively, with far-reaching implications. The editorial staff expounds on any subject related to Black women among its thematic content—from raising children to the racism that one confronts in various ways.

Like all the organizations that I surveyed, and regardless of individual missions among them, one of the goals of *Afroféminas* is to educate the public, including its Black audience, about the historic and current roles of Black women around the world. Whereas most of the Latin American organizations that I studied have a base in a particular country and focus on specific figures from within their respective nations as sources of pride, *Afroféminas* spans the entire globe for its sources of inspiration. While some might see this approach as a challenge to nation-state identities, I see it more as a strategy for surviving in one's new homeland—a reality that is different from discarding notions of nationhood.

From its representations of twentieth-century entertainer and activist Nina Simone to nineteenth-century Yoruba Princess Aina (Lady Sarah Forbes Bonetta), the magazine is replete with images and historical pieces on women of African descent around the world. I learned for the first time that there is such an event as Black History Month in France, with its acronym as BHM, despite the French language in which events occur. Further, if there is a common denominator among Black women across the globe, it is their hair—whether one categorizes it as nappy, kinky, curly, or straight. On the *Afroféminas* website, hair serves as a frequent "contributor," as it drives discussions inviting further reflection on this often-controversial subject surrounding all Black women. In addition, just the image of Black hairstyles frequently speaks volumes, as was the case with the annual hair show in Cameroon. One learns the variety of names in the Spanish language that characterize Black hair. The prominence that hair receives with *Afroféminas* achieves the goal of educating its public, while at the same time offers the sharing of ideas among those who treat their Black hair on a daily basis.

This heterogeneity of materials, processes, and conversations encourages and promotes what I have called diasporic agency, and this also connects to the advocacy of *Afroféminas*' educational outreach. For example, there are regular historical features, both original and shared from the archives of other organizations, such as editorial pieces on current topics and information on the Talleres Afroféminas (Afrofeminist Workshops). Through our interview segments, I learned of the group's frequent travels throughout Spain to conduct workshops on various aspects of Black life there.

One of the major achievements of *Afroféminas* is its ability to cut across borders in ways that many organizations desire to do but have yet to accomplish. For example, among its frequent commenters are immigrants from continental Africa and the whole of Latin America, not to mention Spain. Its many ardent followers and contributors of African descent—whether from Mexico, Chile, or Argentina—participate through the *Afroféminas* website as if they had been waiting for just such an opportunity to connect with other parts of the African diaspora.[23]

Afroféminas is a force in today's digital-savvy world. Yet, how long can an organization continue to grow when it excels because of the extraordinary personal drive of its founder and the zeal of its volunteers? It is already necessary to consider the future of the journal, just as one would any other entity. To the founder's credit, some proactive steps are in the making in this regard, as there is a call for contributors with specific guidelines for those contributions. Many of the current online contributors are volunteers—some with multiple entries, others who volunteer only once. Although easier said than done, some full-time staff would enhance the organization's abilities even further than what one notes today.[24] The workshops, and to a lesser degree the online shopping portals, contribute to bringing the organization closer to its future goals. *Afroféminas* also relies on donations, and one of its latest initiatives is an invitation to have virtual coffee (Ko-fi) with its contributing editors. An online store also generates some revenue for the organization, particularly in its sale of books. Finally, *Afroféminas'* workshops also contribute to the organization's financial health.

Uruguay and Mundo Afro

The online presence of Afro-Uruguayans may come as a surprise. In fact, this is only a natural extension of their collective activism, whose evolution dates far beyond the beginning of the twentieth century. Afro-Uruguay therefore boasts an online presence that is a logical extension of long-term institutional organizing. Further, the more than century-old organizational precedents of entities within Uruguay allowed for a logical transition to NGOs and later to an online presence. Additionally, Afro-Uruguay stands out for its consistent knowledge of and contact with people of African descent around the world, despite the relatively small percentage of Afrodescendants in Uruguay's population. It constitutes yet another example of how a digital presence is transforming the connections among people and, most specifically for my purposes, the ability of Afro-Latin groups to connect with other Black communities around the world.[25]

Mundo Afro (Afro World) is my organization of choice for Uruguay due to its ability to reach large and varied segments of the African diaspora. Moreover, Mundo Afro is arguably the most important organization of African descent in the Southern Cone of the Americas. There is much to admire about it. Initially a print magazine, the entity is now a regional powerhouse with both online publications and community-based organizing. It also comes close to fulfilling the lofty goal of an umbrella organization. This is true in part because Mundo Afro possesses a seriousness of purpose that has everything to do with diaspora agency, and it produces tangible results. Further, one notes a steady, logical progression in its advocacy: from outside government to within it, including with the organization's founder Romero Rodríguez serving as an ambassador and special assistant to the country's president, with particular attention to people of African descent. In 2007, the Inter American Foundation had this to say: "Mundo Afro has evolved since 1988 from its improbable beginning as a magazine into a network recognized worldwide for its effectiveness—at the grassroots and with government at all levels."[26]

Learning of the extensive series of problems that Mundo Afro combats on a regular basis, a reader could close her eyes and assume that she is in the United States or any other country where diasporans are not the majority. These issues include low education attainment, high incarceration rates, affordable housing, and domestic workers' rights. With beginnings as a magazine, the organization has more than a spiritual bond to the magazine *Nuestra Raza* (Our Race) and other Uruguayan publications that date from the early twentieth century and indeed before.[27] The earlier organizations, including the long-standing *Nuestra Raza*, also promoted Black social and political advancement.

The Web presence in Uruguay that was most beneficial to me is more of a network of regional bodies, Organizaciones Mundo Afro (Afro World Organizations), and not the magazine itself. On the other hand, members of Mundo Afro maintain *Facebook* and *Twitter* accounts, and Director Pereira's direct stamp is visible. None of the three social media outlets—the Inter-American Foundation (IAF) website, the *Facebook* page, or the *Twitter* account—contradicts the other, but the *Twitter* feed provides more up-to-date information about what occurs in the Southern Cone in relation to its Afro-Latin people. It also demonstrates knowledge, as does Mundo Afro in general, of people of African descent around the world.

While Mundo Afro tackles systemic racial problems, the organization continues to stress the attainments of Afro-Uruguayans and other people of African descent. This is true to the degree that its annual carnival and, separately, drumming lessons augur well as a propitious site for global tourism, including

Afro-tourism.[28] Moreover, its outreach to other countries and organizations continues to impress, even in this period of digital reach. On a regular basis, Director Pereira tweets his messages about regional happenings and about his listening tours across the Americas and other regions of the globe where people of African descent happen to be. True to the nature of most Afro-Latin organizations, Organizaciones Mundo Afro's goal of educating the public in an effort to stem racism is front and center. A major example of such is the prominence afforded the artist and activist Lágrima Ríos (River of Tears). The group's focus on her confirms its efforts to cherish elders, not just remember the past.[29] Additionally, Mundo Afro's growth is attributable to the hard work of its staff, including its ability to seek funding as an NGO. Further funding comes from the national government, which at times helps with the costs of specific projects like programming of special events and even reports on the needs of Afro-Uruguayans.

Challenges and Lessons

Important to an organization's success is its ability to network beyond national borders—or at least the prospect of doing so in the future. In this regard, *Afroféminas* and AfroAmérica XXI showed the most promise. As I show throughout this chapter, only *Afroféminas* continues to succeed in this goal. There are sporadic citings of AfroAmérica XXI to this day, and this shows some adherence to its key principles. Yet, the organization as a whole is not functional. Mundo Afro reaches far beyond the Southern Cone with its online presence but also with its members traveling around the globe wherever there is a Black presence. They also invite members of other African diaspora communities and from Africa to their country as a means of keeping on top of diaspora happenings. Two cases that stand out are Efuka Longé of the Democratic Republic of the Congo and Angela Davis of the United States. The former arrived in Uruguay at the behest of the organization and is now a major presence there. Angela Davis continues to inspire Black communities around the world, and Mundo Afro proudly hosted her visit. Many more examples are on its *Facebook* page. Some umbrella organizations show efforts of regional networking. That was the case with AfroAmérica XXI and it continues to hold true for Organizaciones Mundo Afro that I analyzed earlier in this text. This networking holds much promise for Afro-Latin

America's ability to reach beyond one region and to connect with the entire African diaspora.

On the other side of digital access is the hard truth that debuting too soon may be a hindrance rather than a blessing. "Build it and they will come" may be true in the entertainment sphere, but in the world of digerati, impatience on the part of viewers keeps this from gradually coming to fruition. This was the case with AfroAmérica XXI, which should have come on the public scene fully formed and not in its infancy. Particularly in eras of fiscal austerity, funding institutions are reluctant to release monies that do not go toward proven entities. All organizations seeking to exist beyond a few years require resources, and as if the problem of resources were not enough, shift in political winds before an organization gets off the ground can be a determining factor in the very continuance of the entity. Partnering with other, more research-advantaged institutions does not constitute a treasonous act of giving in to "them." Instead, reaching out to NGOs, INGOs, and even one's government can be a reasonable step—provided the group takes measures to ensure a degree of autonomy that keeps the organization on path to achieving its goals.

Grit alone cannot power an organization to success. Instead, organizations need the characteristics outlined in the description of IO theory and spelled out in the table in Appendix 2 at the end of this chapter to carry them into the future. Not only are guidelines a must, but so is strong, effective leadership. Far from being authoritarian, strong leadership connotes capable handling of the organization's issues. One finds two good examples of strong leadership in Educafro and *Afroféminas*, but the case of AfroAmérica XXI gives pause to anyone seeking answers about leadership within the group, or indeed to questions about the current strength of the organization. Even when organizations set out to be a group effort with all who are willing as participants in its existence, as in the case of *Wikipedia*, someone or some group is in the background making decisions about content and policies. At some level, even the youngest of online platforms must have an organizational structure if it is to survive beyond its nascent stage. Further, every entity—whether a mom-and-pop grocery store or a huge behemoth like Microsoft—must identify someone ready to take on the helm when the person in charge no longer functions in that role.

Afro-Latin American organizations with online capabilities are both unique and similar to many group entities that made the choice to have an active internet presence. They are alike in most of the struggles—and triumphs—that they face, with the decision of how much to involve social media in their outreach to their constituents. Further, the ageless question of resources plagues these organizations, just as it does non-Afro-Latin groups. As one can see with *Afroféminas*, and with regard to resources, the internet can prove to be one of their greatest assets due to its ability to lessen costs and the time necessary for maintaining contact with the larger public. Interestingly, for three of the organizations, it was never a question of old forms of on-the-ground organization vs. on-the-internet society but rather the two forms working in tandem. Equally interesting is that the internet-born organization *Afroféminas* is working to create a physical presence through lecturing and workshops. It does this while maintaining its original virtual presence.

Conclusion

The groups I studied work within their nations and advocate for the rights of Black people, but many also cultivate links with organizations and individuals elsewhere who are pursuing similar goals. Further, by pointing out their commonalities with the whole of the African diaspora and with Africa itself, they strengthen their ability to effect change. This commonality—the working for the betterment of their people—is an expression of what I have called diaspora agency, an important characteristic of such organizations that might lead us to think differently about the more abstract approach of IO theory.

Revisiting some important, general characteristics of organizations examined by IO theory as expressed in the table in Appendix 2, as well as my own observations as they appear above, I find that it is easier to see how and when Afro-Latin American organizations are at their best. Issues that I examined, such as effective leadership, clear goals, and sufficient resources are aspects of organizations that IO theory addresses in order to gauge the effectiveness of particular organizations. It is important to note, however, that the analysis or conclusion that resulted from this research is not a comment on the worthiness of the organizations that were reviewed. In fact, with their sheer goodwill and drive, the groups impressed me more than at the beginning of my research. This leads me to one truth that stands out and that does not receive adequate treatment with the IO parameters of the table in Appendix 2: the contribution of diaspora agency to the survival, and indeed to the thriving, of an online enterprise. Yet the desire to promote diaspora agency is not enough, since my study also shows that organizations with strong statements in this regard can also fail in their mission. AfroAmérica XXI is the prime example here, since, regardless of a professed investment in transnational Black issues, its website is dormant for all practical purposes, and IO theory offers parameters that can adequately explain its current inert state, as can be seen in Appendix 2. However, the contrasting success of *Afroféminas* also shows that an investment in particular issues can establish strong networks from which resources, volunteers, funding, and even leadership can emerge. It is perhaps no coincidence that AfroAmérica XXI seems to exemplify Scott and Davis's idea of rational or natural systems, whereas *Afroféminas* seems to be more of an open one. It is the energy and dynamism of *Afroféminas'* audience and contributors that seems to be largely responsible for its success, and this energy and dynamism is largely attributable to diaspora agency. In this light, I would suggest that there is room for IO theory to incorporate more studies that focus on smaller organizations whose intent is not to encompass the world or even a region but rather to use online tools to establish networks and alliances from the piece of the globe they call home. This will be particularly relevant for Afro-Latin organizations, whose concerns emerge from highly localized conditions that are nevertheless linked by the historical conditions of the African diaspora.

Appendix 1

1) AfroAmérica XXI: in Colombia, the last update, from 2014, is available at https://prezi.com/8mmovaxwjq34/brochure-afroamerica-xxi/. In Honduras, the last update, from 2017, is available at https://Twitter.com/afroamericaxxi. See analysis in this chapter.

2) *Afroféminas*, Spain: https://afrofeminas.com/. See analysis in this chapter.

3) Asociación de Artistas Ecuatorianos: https://es-la.facebook.com/Asociacion-de-Artistas-Afro-ecuatorianos-1625452351061742/.

4) Asociación Caboverdeana de Ensenada, Argentina: The Cape Verdean Association of Ensenada springs from the Asociación Cultural y Deportiva Caboverdeana (Cape Verdean Cultural and Sport Association). https://www.facebook.com/caboverdeana.deensenada.

5) Asociación Movimiento Nacional por los Derechos Humanos de las Comunidades (National Association Movement for Human Rights in the Communities), Colombia: http://movimientocimarron.org/.

6) Asociación Negra de Defensa y Promoción de los Derechos Humanos (ASONEDH) (Black Association for the Defense and Promotion of Human Rights), Peru: http://asonedhperu.org/

7) Asociación de Residentes Senegaleses en Argentina (Association of Senegalese Residents in Argentina): https://es-la.facebook.com/Asociaci%C3%B3n-De-Residentes-Senegaleses-En-Argentina-476471835855248/.

8) Centro Intercultural Martin Luther King (Martin Luther King Intercultural Center), Bolivia: https://www.facebook.com/pg/CentroInterculturalMartinLutherKing/about/?ref=page_internal https://ganyingo.wordpress.com/.

9) Educafro: https://www.educafro.org.br/site/ See analysis in this chapter.

10) Fundación Afroamiga (Afro Friend Foundation), Venezuela: https://afroamiga.wordpress.com/.

11) Fundación Afromexicana Petra Morga, AC-Mexico: https://www.facebook.com/tere.mojica.1 or https://Twitter.com/teremojica?lang=en pp 67/122.

12) Fundación Bahía Portobello (Portobello Bay Foundation), Panama: fundacionbp.org/

13) Instituto Ganga Zumba (Ganga Zumba Institute), Brazil: https://gangazumbadotorg.wordpress.com/ See also: https://www.cenbrasil.org.br.

14) Instituto de Pesquisas e Estudos Afrobrasileiros (IPEAFRO), Brazil: (Institute for Afro Brazilian Research and Study): http://ipeafro.org.br/.

15) Lumbanga, Chile: https://www.facebook.com/lumbanga/.

16) LUNDU, Peru: https://www.facebook.com/LUNDU.AFROPERUANOS/.

17) Manuel Zapata Olivella Center, Washington, DC, USA: https://www.facebook.com/Manuel-Zapata-Olivella-Center-168022632275/.

18) Mundo Afro, Uruguay: https://es-es.facebook.com/OrganizacionesMundoAfro. See analysis within this chapter.

19) Organización de Desarrollo Étnico Comunitario (ODECO), Honduras: http://odecohn.blogspot.com/p/sobre-nosotros.html.

20) Organización Negra Centroamericana (ONECA) (Black Central American Organization), Honduras: Associated with ODECO, about which SEGIB has much to say.

Appendix 2

The table below extracts, in abbreviated form, some of the key components of data collection to get a sense of the staying power of the four organizations I feature above. Beyond identification of the entity, here I convert my observations into simple "yes" or "no" categories that share a sense of how likely the organization is to carry on into the future. The table is merely a snapshot of what is occurring at the moment of submission of this chapter. The results represent my own assessment of where the health of the organization stands. None of the information for the organizations is etched in stone. The results can change, depending on what steps the organization might be presently undertaking in order to maximize its efforts.

Categories

"Website" refers to whether or not the organization has a current website at the time this chapter was submitted for final publication. "Leader" denotes whether or not the online presence indicates a person or a group that is in charge of implementing decisions for the organization. "Mission" indicates whether or not the group has a clearly defined goal. "Funding" identifies whether or not the group has the *current* monetary resources to carry out its basic mission. "Dialogue" ascertains whether or not the public has the ability to engage in public or private conversations with the group. Recognizing that often groups are under-resourced and lack the ability to make daily changes to

Table 6.1. Afro-Latinx organizations online

Name	Website	Leader	Mission	Funding	Dialogue	Updates
AfroAmérica XXI	No	No	Yes	No	No	No
Afroféminas	Yes	Yes	Yes	No	Yes	Yes
Educafro	Yes	Yes	Yes	Yes	Yes	Yes
Organizaciones Mundo Afro	Yes	Yes	Yes	Yes	Yes	Yes

their websites, "Updates" refers to whether or not the organization has made any changes to the website over the last two years.

Notes

1. See Ellis, "The Organizational Turn," 14.

2. Shaw, *Cooperation*; Vaillant et al., "Hacia una política," 1–4.

3. Covin, *Unified*, 157–87.

4. See Scott and Davis, *Organizations and Organizing*.

5. Ibid., 63.

6. Arriaga, Sancho Caparrini, and Suárez, "Modeling"; Beverungen, "The Organizational Powers"; Powell et al., "Institutional Analysis"; Sommerer and Talberg, "Diffusion."

7. Powell et al., 308.

8. Marielle Franco was a political activist whom some believe died at the hands of the government. Further, many insist that her lesbian identity played a part in her killing.

9. The public sharing of my research in progress began with a series of lectures I conducted in Honduras and Guatemala in February 2016 under the auspices of the State Department of the United States. See: Captain, "Civil Rights."

10. SEGIB was formed in 2005 as "an international support organisation for 22 countries that make up the Ibero-American community." Its headquarters is in Spain. See SEGIB, "Who We Are."

11. I decided to select only twenty organizations because they had common elements, such as self-identification as Afro-Latin organizations, and/or were associated with countries where Afrodescendant organizations were strong actors. For an extensive list of Afro-Latin Organizations, see SEGIB, *Organizaciones*.

12. The organization sometimes uses the Arabic numerals 21 as part of its name rather than the Roman numerals XXI. In addition, some publications list its beginning as 1996.

13. Parentheses in the original, translation mine. See Educafro, "Conheça Educafro."

14. Liberation theology is a concept that one associates with one of its major proponents: Peruvian priest, educator, and activist Gustavo Gutiérrez. His 1971 book *Teología de la liberación* gave name to the practice. The book is a living document in that Father Gutiérrez constantly updates it as part of a dialogue with his readers. For pragmatic reasons, however, I cite the translation of 1988. See Gutiérrez, *A Theology*.

15. While I focus on Educafro, entities with a base in Candomblé or Umbanda, with their decidedly African roots, are other possible studies.

16. Translation is mine. See AfroAmérica XXI, "Quiénes."

17. AfroAmérica XX, *Compendio*, 13.

18. See footnote 89 on page 35 of SEGIB, *Organizaciones*.

19. In addition, not to take away from Epsy Campbell's stunning electoral achievement, it bears mentioning that she is the sister of Shirley Campbell Barr, whom I briefly feature here. See AfroAmérica XXI, "Costa Rica."

20. Captain, "West African Migrants"; Sow, "Diásporas."

21. See Afroféminas, "About Us."

22. The title of the event in Spanish was "Primera Cumbre de Lideresas Afro," and the event

took place in Managua, Nicaragua, June 26–28. Although the "first" summit for most Black Latin American groups occurred decades ago, this conference supporting Latin American women of African descent was a momentous event, as some of its organizers let me know during my aforementioned State Department trips in 2016.

23. This was taken from digital snapshots of readers and contributors that I compiled in early 2017 and then later in the year. The persons who carried on dialogues with *Afroféminas* were Afro-Mexican Ricardo Martinez and Afro-Chilean Mercedes Argudín Pacheco, as well as two Afro-Argentines, Irene Ortiz Teixeira and Miriam Victoria Gomes. However, the viewer will often find comments from other regions of Latin America as well as the continent of Africa.

24. In our interview sequence, Torres expressed a desire to expand the staff, and we briefly discussed the limited resources available to *Afroféminas*.

25. Andrews, *Blackness*; Jackson, "The Black Writer"; Lewis, *Afro-Uruguayan*; Persico, "Afro-Uruguayan Culture"; Rodríguez, *Mbundo Malungo*; Rout, *The African Experience*; Young, "The New Voices."

26. Inter-American Foundation, "Afro-Latinos."

27. Rodríguez, *Mbundo Malungo*, 108–14.

28. Andrews, *Blackness*, 112–40.

29. Ríos, "La llamada."

Bibliography

AfroAmérica XXI. *Compendio normativo regional afrodescendiente de América Latina*, 2009. http://www.afroamerica21.com/uploads/files/1p.pdf.

———. "Costa Rica fortalece con inclusión su sistema democrático." *Facebook*, April 9, 2018. https://www.facebook.com/xxiafroamericaxxi/?hc_ref=ARTH_4vSplqQraiBE6ArKxnAY9FwAXkWnx_2lwUclkSkv5N_bJhOHpS2BgQjllzOZ-s&fref=nf.

———. "¿Quiénes somos?" http://www.afroamerica21.com/.

Afrocubaweb.com.

Afroféminas, "About Us." Accessed April 22, 2020. https://afrofeminas.com/.

Andrews, George Reid. *Blackness in the White Nation: A History of Afro-Uruguay*. Chapel Hill: University of North Carolina Press, 2010.

Arriaga, Eduard. A., Fernando Sancho Caparrini, and Juan Luis Suárez. "Modeling Afro-Latin American Artistic Representations in Topic Maps: Cuba's Prominence in Latin American Discourse," *Digital Humanities Quarterly* 7, no. 1 (2013).

Barkin, J. S. *International Organization: Theories and Institutions*. New York: Palgrave Macmillan, 2013.

Barnett, M., and M. Finnemore. *Rules for the World: International Organizations in Global Politics*. Ithaca, NY: Cornell University Press, 2004.

Beverungen, A., Timon Beyes, and Lisa Conrad. "The Organizational Powers of (Digital) Media." Special issue *Organization* 26, no. 5 (2019): 621–35.

Captain, Yvonne. "Civil Rights Movements in the U.S. and in Afro-Latin America: A Suggested Comparative Framework." Paper presented in Honduras and Guatemala, 2016. https://yvonnecaptain.com/lectures-interviews/.

———. "West African Migrants in Spain: Human Factors and Emerging International Policy." *International Journal of Interdisciplinary Social Sciences* 3, no. 10 (2009): 61–68.

Covin, David. *The Unified Black Movement in Brazil: 1978–2002.* Jefferson: McFarland & Company, 2006.

Educafro. "Conheça Educafro." Accessed April 22, 2020. http://www.educafro.org.br/site/.

Ellis, David. "The Organizational Turn in International Organization Theory." *Journal of International Organizations Studies* 1, no. 1 (2010): 11–28.

de la Fuente, Alejandro, and George Reid Andrews. *Afro-Latin American Studies: An Introduction.* Cambridge, UK: Cambridge University Press, 2018.

Gutiérrez, Gustavo. *A Theology of Liberation: History, Politics and Salvation.* Translated by Sister Caridad Inda and John Eaglson. Maryknoll, NY: Orbis Books, 1988.

Hurd, I. F. "Choices and Methods in the Study of International Organizations." *Journal of International Organization Studies* 2 (2011). http://journal-iostudies.org/node/31.

Instituto Brasileiro de Geografia e Estatística (IBGE). http://censo2010.ibge.gov.br/apps/atlas/.

Inter-American Foundation (IAF). "Afro-Latinos Count Themselves In." Accessed April 20, 2020. https://www.iaf.gov/content/50th-anniversary/afro-latinos-count-themselves-in/.

Jackson, Richard L. "The Black Writer, the Black Press, and the Black Diaspora in Uruguay." In *Black Writers in Latin America.* Albuquerque: University of New Mexico Press, 1979: 93–111.

Lewis, Marvin A. *Afro-Uruguayan Literature: Post-Colonial Perspectives.* Lewisburg: Bucknell University Press, 2003.

Mina Aragón, William. *Manuel Zapata Olivella. Un legado Intercultural.* Bogotá: Fundación Universitaria de Popayán; Ediciones desde abajo, 2016.

Organizaciones Mundo Afro. https://www.facebook.com/OrganizacionesMundoAfro/ and https://twitter.com/mundo_afro_uy.

Pease, Kelly-Kate S. *International Organizations.* 5th ed. Boston: Longman, 2012.

Persico, Melva. "Afro-Uruguayan Culture and Legitimation: Candombe and Poetry." In *Black Writing, Culture, and the State in Latin America*, edited by Jerome Branche, 213–36. Nashville, TN: Vanderbilt University Press, 2015.

Powell, Walter W., Achim Oberg, Valeska Korff, Carrie Oelberger, and Karina Kloos. "Institutional Analysis in a Digital Era: Mechanisms and Methods to Understand Emerging Fields." In *New Themes in Institutional Analysis: Topics and Issues from European Research*, edited by Georg Krücken, Carmelo Mazza, Renate E Meyer, and Peter Walgenbach: 1–62. Cheltenham, UK: Edward Elgar Publishers, 2017.

Ríos, Lágrima. "La llamada." Accessed April 22, 2020. https://www.youtube.com/watch?v=qQFE9I4MDAQ.

Rodríguez, Romero Jorge. *Mbundo Malungo a Mundele: Historia del movimiento afrouruguayo y sus alternativas de desarrollo.* Montevideo: Rosebud Ediciones, 2006.

Rout, Leslie B. *The African Experience in Spanish America, 1502 to the Present Day.* Cambridge, UK: Cambridge University Press, 1976.

Scott, W. Richard, and Gerald F. Davis. *Organizations and Organizing: Rational, Natural and Open System Perspectives.* Upper Saddle River, NJ: Pearson Prentice Hall, 2007.

Secretaría General Iberoamericana (SEGIB). *Organizaciones de la población afro-descendiente de América Latina* 2016. http://segib.org/wp-content/uploads/Organizaciones-Poblacion-Afrodescendiente-ESP-Baja.pdf.

———. "Who We Are." Accessed April 22, 2020. https://www.segib.org/en/who-we-are/.

Shaw, Carolyn M. *Cooperation, Conflict and Consensus in the Organization of American States.* New York: Palgrave Macmillan, 2004.

Sommerer, Thomas, and Jonas Talberg. "Diffusion across International Organizations: Connectivity and Convergence." *International Organization* 73, no. 2 (Spring 2019): 399–433.

Sow, Papa. "Diásporas africanas y mundialización: De la representación histórica a la toma de conciencia." In África *en Diáspora. Movimientos de población y políticas estatales*, edited by Ferrán Iniesta, 135–50. Barcelona: Fundación CIDOB, 2007.

Vaillant, Marcel, Julio Berlinski, Honorio Kume, and Guida Piani. "Hacia una política comercial común del Mercosur." *Serie/Brief* 4. Montevideo: Red de Investigaciones Económicas del MERCOSUR, 2006.

Young, Caroll. "The New Voices of Afro-Uruguay" *Afro-Hispanic Review* 14, no. 1 (1995): 58–64.

7

Between Analog and Digital Activism in Afro-Colombia

Interview with Yancy Castillo and Dora Inés Vivanco

EDUARD ARRIAGA AND ANDRÉS VILLAR

TRANSLATED BY EDUARD ARRIAGA AND ANDRÉS VILLAR

Yancy Castillo and Dora Inés Vivanco are, respectively, coordinator of communications and coordinator of infancy and institutional projects and the technical team at CNOA, Conferencia Nacional de Organizaciones Afrocolombianas (National Assembly of Afro-Colombian Organizations) in Bogotá, Colombia.[1] CNOA emerged from an initial meeting of Afro-Colombian organizations in 2002 and since then has advocated for more than 270 Afrodescendant groups dealing with issues such as woman and youth rights and people displaced by violence.

*   *   *

1. What place do digital tools have In CNOA's practice and in the development of its mission (in contrast to analogous and more traditional tools)?

As of the organization's 2013–2017 strategic plan, the communications area was strengthened and deemed a crucial strategic line for the developing content. In turn, this prompted the acquisition of new technologies and means to narrate, both by the technical team and the regional *mingas*[2] wanting to communicate and reach diverse audiences. Since then, the use of digital tools has been fundamental to the development of strategic actions to communicate with and educate communities beyond the groups that are part of the organization [CNOA].

2. What are the most useful features that digital tools bring to your practice?

The content that CNOA wants to communicate using digital tools is developed by, and in conjunction with, the target audience. This means that our final products for digital communication have been approved by the people, especially Afro-Colombian people, and their wish to communicate. In this sense, the Afro-Colombian peoples see themselves represented, and therefore replicate that representation within the interested communities—for example, the pedagogical material of stories told by Afro-Colombian children that is gathered in *Leilani*, our most recent e-book, has been used not only by CNOA member organizations in their own territories, but also by teachers in schools, by other organizations, and by government agencies who want to work with diverse ethnic populations on issues of self-recognition.

3. What are the effects (positive and negative) of the use of digital tools in your culture (local, regional, national, ethnic, etc.)?

Positive effects: CNOA is one of the Afro-Colombian social organizations most concerned with making appropriate use of digital tools. We have a well-designed, measurable, and applicable digital strategy connected to diverse audiences ranging from communities with limited access to digital tools and networks, to those who have unlimited access, including students, researchers, international partners, and other professionals interested in our issues.

Negative effects: Colombia does not have internet coverage in all of the national territory, which means that not all of the Afrodescendant population has access to CNOA's digital content. Also we understand that due to the lack of digital literacy and to economic constraints, among other factors, not all Afrodescendant communities have access to digital tools. However, with those barriers in mind, CNOA sends the materials in an analog format to the regional *mingas* so that the information can be shared.

We see the digital as a complement to what we do. Social networks are to inform and communicate, to keep people in touch.

4. Does the digital help connect or reconnect communities identified and/or self-identified as belonging to the African diaspora (among themselves and with communities in the African continent)? In case your answer is negative, why?

The access to digital tools allows us to generate political, educational, social, and religious influence. This is something shown by the increasing number of followers on our social networks, people of the Afro-Colombian movement who share our content, showing that they are interested. This, the daily visits to our web page, and the sharing of links to CNOA's site converging or consolidating information also shows that someone consumes our content. It is true that communication and the strengthening of discourse about Afro-Colombian topics occurs first among those who work and live in the African diaspora, but the world is digitally connected, and we cannot be oblivious to advances and new ways of communicating and educating ourselves.

5. Why do you think that establishing and/or maintaining connections between these Afro-diasporic communities is important, particularly in the so-called digital age?

It is vital to know the needs of Afro-diasporic communities—what they lack and what their realities are in terms of rights—in order to generate the required transformations. Those digital connections you refer to allow us to change the realities of these communities. For example, many types of violence suffered by Afrodescendant communities in Colombia because of the armed conflict and the implementation of the peace agreements have been made visible quickly with the aid of digital tools and networks. These communities have used cellphones to record situations of violence and to distribute the media through platforms such as WhatsApp and other social networks. With such methods, injustices are denounced directly and an impact is made even before national social organizations, the media, the government, and international institutions arrive to resolve the issue. For these reasons, it is vital to maintain and increase the connections between Afrodescendant/Afro-Colombian communities and the digital.

6. What is the role played by nostalgic and utopian conceptions in the development of digital projects that try to re-connect and make visible Afrodescendant attributes?

The point of departure for our projects, whether analog or digital, is respect for the ancestral wisdom of Afrodescendant peoples. We have found, however, that many of the traditional customs of these communities have disappeared because of a lack of systematization, or because elderly people, who are responsible for transmitting these customs or processes to the new generations, are dying. Using digital tools and applications allows us to foster processes of memory or to create memory when there is none, so that we can record and disseminate these memories to the current and future generations who create meaning in both digital and analog worlds.

7. Who is in charge of programming, designing, hosting, and technical support for your project?

For the programming and hosting we use a company in Bogotá that provides services tailored specifically to social organizations.

We have three professionals dedicated to technical support in communications. One of them is a female designer who is responsible for the design, the illustrations, the videos, and the animations uploaded to the CNOA webpage. Another woman is in charge of the articles, and of the uploading of all information to the web and incorporating it into CNOA's digital strategy, which consists of promoting particular content that will generate traffic on social networks or visits to the webpage. Our current strategy also includes encouraging our allies to participate more actively in generating content, although at this moment they do so from their territories by means of *Huellas de Africanía*, our program on virtual radio that is associated with the University of Rosario's (Bogotá) extension programs.

8. What impact does the incorporation of those local/global agents have in the development of your project?

CNOA would have no reason to exist without the incorporation of local actors—grassroots organizations, community councils, and male or female leaders in the different territories. In their absence, CNOA's work would lack a rationale for being, since it is with them and for them that we develop projects in accordance with CNOA's strategic interests. The technical team takes care of these processes in the communities and fortifies capacities available at different levels so as to better Afro-Colombian peoples' quality of life.

Global actors are allied to CNOA's by means of financing—acquired through calls for funding—that helps strengthen these dynamics at the local level, and through their impact on public policy and in other realms in which decisions that affect the Afrodescendant population are made.

9. What kind of infrastructure do you use to develop your project, whereby infrastructure is understood as any mechanism or method, in addition to computers, involved in carrying out a project?

The structure takes shape as initiatives are designed and developed according to requirements and proposals put forward by the technical team and the *mingas* in the territories. This is done taking into consideration, among other things, human talent, equipment, and materials.

10. Do you take into consideration connections between software, hardware, work, and material resources when you design your digital projects?

Without a doubt. Nevertheless, we start with the forms of communication used by a given population in order to generate digital projects. To clarify: CNOA strives to systematize all projects as video-memories; however, not every project results in a digital product. The latter are realized by including the people who co-operate with the design process.

11. What benefits and challenges do you find in the term "Afro-digital," particularly if you reflect on your own practice?

I find "Afro-digital" useful as long as the different digital strategies create a platform in which one can find all the processes having to do with the African diaspora. However, it can also be read as a term that does not adhere to global digital dynamics. The term itself calls for the recognition of the particularities of Afro people in the territories, the capacities already available, and the dynamics of usage by the population. In this way, instead of pigeonholing, the label can give credence to the diverse ways of generating content in order to connect with Afro realities and with a wider public.

12. Afro-digital connections suggests an expansive terrain of possibilities that perhaps could not be achieved otherwise. What are some of the challenges in establishing such digital connections?

One of the challenges is creating formats and contents that connect with people, and that recognize the reality of the territories and especially the diversity of the Afro population, because there is a risk of homogenizing an audience that consumes digital media. The challenge here is that different audiences will access the content and use it in various ways—for example, boys and girls might read e-books, or seniors might view inter-generational videos.

13. Have you heard of the concept "digital humanities"?

Yes.

14. What is the role of your project in creating knowledge and in helping us to re-think knowledge creation and dissemination?

We seek to generate changes in the imaginary with respect to Afro-Colombian peoples by using pedagogy bringing to light issues of racism and discrimination, which are social problems that must be eradicated. We also highlight the contributions of Afro-Colombian peoples to the construction of the nation, striving to give a more complete x-ray of this pluri-ethnic and multicultural country, as it is described in the Colombian Political Constitution. This will imply giving a face to histories that have not been told; histories made invisible in which Afro-Colombians are also protagonists; histories that go beyond the scenes of servitude and entertainment to which society has tried to limit them.

15. What would be the role of digital tools in making visible and overcoming racism?

Their role is fundamental for deconstructing knowledges founded on racialization and stereotyping, and for constructing learning and knowledges that acquire significance as they are understood to be part of the richness accessed through the understanding of diversity. The myth of *mestizaje*[3] and equality has resulted in the homogenization of knowledge, beauty, and what is understood as the good. Such conceptions leave out Afro-Colombian peoples as racialized, impoverished, and discriminated against in different social fields. Digital tools help us demolish these stereotypes and make visible Afro peoples from other perspectives: how they have contributed to politics, the economy, science, the arts, pedagogy, all of this from their own worldview and from representations constitutive of diversity. This would show that diversity is part of the nation's wealth, and that one must not fear the unknown. One must fight against racism in places such as schools, where boys and girls are the most affected, because racism permeates the construction of identity. Digital tools will continue to be an important means for conveying videos, music, histories, e-books, and other materials we create for diverse audiences in different contexts.

16. What is your project's target audience?

Our digital projects are aimed at different types of audiences. They are created with the clear intention of defining the messages, times, participants, and diversity of voices we would like represented. With this in mind, and depending on the expected result, different areas of our organization participate in the creative processes, but always in coordination with the area of communications. For example, women's videos or infographics about their political participation are aimed at Afro-Colombian women, always seeking to make visible the importance of intergenerational dialogues; e-books, cartoons, and pedagogical videos for self-recognition are aimed at children, but complementary material is also available for adults to guide children in this process; videos for advocacy, development plans, censuses, and other similar materials are focused on young adults, who participate in different scenarios of local action, etc. We understand that our work entails generating the greatest possible impact, always working in an articulated manner as a team and using the resources we have.

17. How do digital tools affect identity, ethnic affiliation, the notion of race, etc., and how is this apparent in your practice?

In our case, we always consider the possibility of generating positive impacts. That is, we strive to guarantee the preservation and visibility of diverse cultural elements such as Creole languages (through translation of videos, using them in the songs, etc.); to reaffirm processes of identity, or what it means to be Afro-Colombian, as a way to eradicate racist and discriminatory practices in different scenarios: work, school, politics, aesthetics, etc. The projects we create involve a process of careful design, which is always done collectively, seeking to portray the elements that are part of our history, our culture, and our identities in a dignified and respectful manner. That is basic for our organization and for the development of digital projects.

18. What is the idea of the human that is at the core of your projects? Who is the human you are trying to target by using digital media?

We understand that the human being is one. Diverse, yes, but one. We also understand that technology must be a means to connect our humanity, to reconnect and tear down barriers of distance, and to enhance voices of protest and defense, and voices that propose. The digital cannot overcome our sense of dignity, since it reflects both the best and the worst of human beings. Our goal will always be to reflect the best of the human being, of the Afro-Colombian people.

19. How did the idea of creating digital projects by the organization come to life? What do you expect to achieve with these and other related projects?

The idea of using digital tools arises from the need to reach various audiences, to connect people, to break down the barriers of distance in order to communicate, and to send our messages to many corners of the country where the Afro-Colombian people live, where issues of security limit the possibility of physical access. But it also came about as a way to learn how to use technological resources so as to innovate and create pedagogical material that allows us to explore different alternatives of communication.

Notes

1. https://convergenciacnoa.org/.

2. *Minga* is a word used by Indigenous and Black communities to refer to a type of traditional collective group formed to tackle an initiative. In the case of CNOA, the groups get together to fight racism in the Colombian context. The word is derived from the Quechua word *minka*. See https://en.wikipedia.org/wiki/Communal_work and https://en.wiktionary.org/wiki/mink%27a.

3. The term *mestizaje*, which has a complex history, can refer to both biological and cultural hybridity. It was used in many Latin American countries during the twentieth century as an ideological tool to justify narratives of national unity and homogeneity. See https://en.wikipedia.org/wiki/Mestizo and note 6 in chapter 8.

8

Toward the Creation of an Afro-Argentine Digital Archive in the Cape Verdean Association of Buenos Aires

MARÍA CECILIA MARTINO

The Cape Verdean Society,[1] which is located in the south of greater Buenos Aires, is a mutual-aid entity that was established in 1932 with the goal of creating links between Cape Verdean immigrants and the local population, and today its membership is composed mostly of those immigrants' descendants. In this essay I will use a historical-ethnographic perspective to analyze the process of digitizing texts and image material related to the society, primarily photographs and documents. This process of digitization preceded and has been done alongside a set of initiatives that converged in the project of organizing a digital archive in the Cape Verdean institution of Dock Sud, which is in its early stage. The archive's objective is to organize, conserve, and give value to a heterogeneous group of documents[2] that testify to a historical and continuing Cape Verdean-Argentinian presence in Argentina. The project began in 2016 by compiling and organizing different institutional documents that had remained in disarray and in a variable state of conservation. Some of these documents were obtained from the members' personal collections, others were brought from Cape Verde,[3] and some were rescued from boxes, furniture in which they had been stored or stashed away, and shelves belonging to the society.

Since the late nineteenth century and throughout most of the twentieth century, Argentina consolidated a national narrative that highlighted an image of the nation based on whiteness. This representation has been reproduced at different levels: by the state, in the discourse of the elites, in everyday interactions, and in national metaphors such as the "melting pot" that emphasize the presence of (Euro-descendant) immigrants as agents of social progress.

This hegemonic narrative refers to the progressive *disappearance* and absence of Afrodescendants and Indigenous people at the core of the Argentinian nation.[4] For this reason, it is generally supposed that few photographs and documents exist about African descendants in Argentina, a visual imaginary that, not by chance, coincides with the national hegemonic narrative. These photographs, most of which remained concealed within domestic spaces, accompanied and reflected a process of *social whitening* that occurred throughout most of the twentieth century[5] and which generated an apparent absence of documentary evidence about Afrodescendants, a "blindness" about the processes of *mestizaje* that makes it difficult to visualize non-whites in daily life.[6] If, however, we look more closely, we can see how photographs and written documents played an important role in some of these families. Among Argentinian-Cape Verdeans, images and letters helped reconnect relatives inside and outside the country. With these documents, people demonstrated an interest in maintaining these ties at the same time that photographs helped re-create these social links when the people were physically absent.

The project of creating an Afro-Argentine digital archive attempts to halt this gradual process of invisibility. However, as we shall see in this essay, reverting an entrenched narrative is neither spontaneous nor easy. In effect, one encounters a series of problems that refer, in broad terms, to issues of how to represent these people and by what means. As Livio Sansone notes, it becomes difficult to find an easy answer to these types of questions when the state intervenes in the production of cultures and identities at the same time that subaltern groups fight for recognition.[7] In Buenos Aires, the way in which the state represents Afrodescendants differs from how these groups define themselves. On the one hand, the tendency of the Afro-activist sphere toward a racialization of identities—and the dynamics assumed by the identities in these contexts—creates a tension with the "descent principle" that these associations sought to legitimize by appealing to the category of "Afrodescendants." On the other hand, when incorporated into public policies, the combination of these principles (race and descent) strengthens different representations about

Blackness in Argentina and establishes selective logics that privilege some ways of being Afrodescendant over others, or redirects this presence to the traditional national narrative about the absence of properly Argentine Blacks.[8]

This leads to other questions about the politics of representation that I will address in this essay, such as: How can one label or name an archive without limiting any potential links with other Afrodescendant collectives and activists? How can one name an archive that makes visible the presence of Afrodescendants across the nation? And finally, how is it possible to stimulate the participation and collective work of young people? In order to respond to these questions with answers that were not closed or definitive, it was important to create an archive that reflected a broader Afrodescendant heritage. I will concentrate on some activities that highlight how digital technologies have affected associative and communitarian practices linked to the project.

The archive is currently in its initial stages, which elicits a series of issues that are not yet fully defined but that show the complexity inherent in an initial classification of documents about Afrodescendants in Argentina. What will become apparent throughout this essay is that this first re-organization involves issues that are not only technical but also fundamentally political. Moreover, I seek to problematize a set of situations elicited by the process of digitization itself, which include the reconfigurations of identity that I will analyze and that are at play when digitized images and documents circulate *outside* the domestic spaces or storage boxes of the Cape Verdean association of Dock Sud. In such cases, I will examine how some photographs and documentary information "mediate" between different generations of Argentinian-Cape-Verdeans and explore the meanings they have for each of these groups and the effects generated in the forms of self-representations they affirm. Some of these digitized photographs are projected at public homages, while others are uploaded and shared on social networks, and, on certain occasions, their mobilization across this circuit facilitates their appropriation by elements of the state committed to the politics of recognizing Afrodescendant individuals and groups. As Sansone has noted, the new technologies of communication have a profound effect on the construction of memory as it is articulated with the process of formulating identities. Ludmila da Silvia Catela suggests that "if memories cultivate us in terms of identity, and we, in turn, shape them, it is critical to observe with what materials, when, and how these memories are formed."[9] In response to this suggestion, in the following section I will explore

a series of theoretical and methodological perspectives that will help me examine how digital technologies mediate and affect specific social relations and
the process of constructing memories made invisible by the state.

Images, Technologies, and Representation

I begin with Elisenda Ardèvol's suggestion that a continuum of practices and
interactions between online and offline contexts expresses the imbrication of
virtual and non-virtual visual codes in our worlds.[10] In the passages between
virtual and non-virtual contexts, the meaning given to photographs and written documents is re-contextualized, transforming their meanings.

Therefore, rather than concentrating on the particular role played by digital
technology, I will analyze the structure constituted by technologies, discourses,
and practices that come together in specific situations, such as contexts of increasing political activism by people of African descent. In other words, I will
explore what people do with technology, how they appropriate it, and for what
projects, be they personal, cultural, social, local, or global.[11] As has been noted
by some authors,[12] what is visual has generally been linked to the study of
representation. This perspective will be complemented by social and cultural
practices related to the production, circulation, and appropriation of images,
which are important dimensions of an ethnographic analysis that seeks to capture the relationships between these different levels in the visual economy.[13]
With this in mind, I will refer to a meaning of "mediation" that goes beyond the
notion of representation and whose sense focuses on the transformations that
take place when relations are established between objects and individuals.[14]
That is, photographic instruments and images do more than represent reality,
given that the devices capture some external realities (whether now or in the
past) and so make them present in particular ways.[15] This latter point is significant in a country such as Argentina, which has continued to sustain a narrative
based on a national imaginary proclaiming a white-European heritage about
the *disappearance* of people of African descent. This imaginary is currently
undergoing significant transformations as Afrodescendant organizations lead
a struggle for visibility and against racism and exclusion.[16]

An analysis of "situational contexts"[17] will help visualize the dynamics in
which images and digitized archives participate: activating memories, allow-
ing viewers to imagine situations they have not lived, and divulging presences

made invisible by the state. In what follows, I will briefly go over dilemmas and challenges that emerged at the moment of naming the archival project.

"Naming" Social Collectives in the Context of *Porteño* "Multiculturalism"[18]

As an initial step of classification, the naming of an archive provides a basic grounding for the topics that will direct and frame the categories established within the archive itself. As noted by Caggiano, social classifications are fundamental "because their limits perform critical organizational work"[19]; they are therefore not innocuous, since they directly affect the formation of social imaginaries.[20] In Claude Lévi-Strauss's terms, a name configures a "memory" that renders a particular strategy for organizing and visualizing the social world.[21] To this, one can add the difficulty of naming a dynamic process characterized by constant redefinition. In Buenos Aires, the activism enacted by African descendants since the second half of 1990 has reconsidered possibilities for action and modes of self-determination. Some of these actions feed on conflictive political junctures in which the members of the Cape Verdean Society of Dock Sud fight to establish the legitimacy of their ancestry and their presence in the country.

Given these dilemmas, the most immediate way to frame the present archival project is through an "Argentinian-Cape Verdean" designation (*voz*), given that it has the advantage of circumscribing the thematic specificity of the archive (it is ultimately an initiative by the Cape Verdean Society of Dock Sud). Naming it after this particular group would facilitate connecting the archive to the state of Cape Verde, which promotes relations with communities of Cape Verdean emigrants and their descendants in the diaspora. This is an important aspect of the project, since the archive seeks to establish contacts and agreements with the African islands' state archives, which are also undergoing a similar process of digitization. Because of this, giving the archive a name that references the dual Cape Verdean and Argentinian national roots establishes more explicit contact points between these two nations.

However, strengthening the transnational relevance of this membership— of the properly Cape Verdean diaspora—leaves out other collectives of Afro-Argentinian activists who are currently establishing significant articulations. In this regard, the *voz* "Afro-Argentine" has the potential to incorporate other groups into a politically significant category that underlines the national membership of the Argentine-Cape Verdeans.[22]

By contrast, the term Afrodescendant, conceived in the context of the 2001 Durban Conference against Racism,[23] is a slippery concept[24] that in Argentina lacks effective appropriation by the groups and individuals it is supposed to represent. Its use by state entities, however, is much more spontaneous and immediate, although in specific situations and contexts its usage implies that Afrodescendants are fundamentally foreign.[25] As noted by Eduard Arriaga, "the questions of identity, patrimony, representation, and self-representation continue to encircle subjects already classified, recognized, and self-recognized within this global category."[26] I will initially refer to "Afro-Argentines" during the initial stages of my analysis and later specify descriptors that will help highlight the emphasis given the Argentinian-Cape Verdean collective.

Periods and Periodization

In what follows I will explore the archive's periodization by examining the records of the Cape Verdean institution of Dock Sud, which were the first set of documents to be digitized. As noted in a previous study,[27] the records reflect both the conflicts and the agreements that, through writing, have been fixed in procedures that are currently used as a point of reference, since they constitute important precedents. The records provide a yearly account from 1932 to the present, with several converging topics of history: local (the neighborhood), national (Argentina), and transnational (Cape Verde, Brazil, Portugal, and the United States). In line with this crossing of levels, as a first step in organizing the documents I will be grouping them chronologically into three periods: 1930–1950, 1951–1970, and 1971–1990.

Broadly speaking, the first period brings together the issues related to the founding of the institution. At the local level, it presents the normative pillars, rules, and moral values that will guide its members, and we begin to glimpse the work of cultural promotion that the institution will carry out in the neighborhood and beyond. It shows relationships with other clubs and associations, especially Portuguese institutions and Cape Verdean Ensenada, in a context characterized by strong ties in the country. As for the transnational links: there are records of a large amount of correspondence with Cape Verdeans residing in the islands and in other countries and the circulation of newspapers and news stimulated by the active press of the archipelago.

The second period, from 1951 to 1970, reflects the debates on what space to give young people who arrived in Argentina from the Cape Verde islands in 1947, some of whom came together in the group "Cape Verdean Youth," which disputed the meanings upheld by the leaders of the association in relation to its European-Portuguese origin.[28] Regarding the transnational level: correspondence with Cape Verde continues, especially through the press organizations of the archipelago. Links are established with representatives of the PAIGC[29] Regional Committee, a local body founded during this period to disseminate political news about the islands.[30]

Finally, in the third period, the records narrate the events unleashed by the independence of the islands (1975). They mention the discussions and the different positions that marked this political event. At that moment, the records captured the activities carried out by the institution at the local level: organizing numerous meetings in Dock Sud, Ensenada, and the city of Buenos Aires. In terms of transnational links, during this period trips are organized to the archipelago, and a consular representation of Cape Verde is established in the city of Buenos Aires.

Documents in the records for the 1980s and 1990s show that after independence the institution will continue to define initiatives aimed at attracting the participation of the immigrants' descendants and expanding their links with local institutions. Transnational links unfold in two ways: on the one hand, relations with the Cape Verde islands are strengthened by the trips to Cape Verde that the descendants begin to make in the context of a favorable exchange rate with the US dollar;[31] on the other hand, relations are established with Afrodescendant organizations in other countries, mainly the United States.

This periodization, and the proposed local, national, and transnational levels, can also be implemented in the classification of photographic documents that portray different circumstances mentioned in the records.

As we shall see in more detail in what follows, the Cape Verdean association has been undergoing a process of institutional redefinition that has aligned it with the claims of Afrodescendant groups in other places. In turn, this has problematized the association's institutional memory in different ways. Because of this, I consider that it is important to give some account of this thematic and political redefinition, as suggested by the classification that has been proposed for the archive, and to examine the reconfiguration of memories as they are expressed by means of new digital devices (videos, photographs, digital documentaries, and social networks) used to organize past association events.

A Brief History of the Links between Cape Verdeans and Portuguese in Buenos Aires

The Cape Verde islands were occupied and colonized by Portugal for five centuries by means of a sustained process of miscegenation that established a notion of "cultural particularity" distinct from that of continental Africa. This cultural distance began to be redefined during independence, when Amílcar Cabral sought to re-create a historical memory that referred to the close connections with the African mainland during the slave trade, in which Cape Verde played a central role.[32] This memory has not been emphasized by the people who have emigrated from Cape Verde to Argentina throughout the years[33] and is only now being reassessed by the newer generations born in the latter country.

In light of the identity politics that developed in the region under the paradigm of multiculturalism, the context for the mobilization of different Afrodescendant groups in Argentina during the second half of the 1990s strengthened an interpretation that, unlike in the previous periods, emphasized Amílcar Cabral's role in Cape Verde's independence and especially his links with a pan-Africanism that highlights Guinea-Bissau's central role in the process of independence.[34]

In what follows I will analyze how, in form and in content, the new modes commemorating Cabral's assassination and the islands' independence (new in that they incorporate tools such as video cameras, filmic material, and digitized photographs) stimulate novel and strengthened self-representations among the youngest generation of Cape Verdean-Argentinians. Although concepts of "form" and "content" cannot be completely separated, at first I will describe how these videos are elaborated and edited and later I will concentrate my attention on the contexts of their reception as framed by the homages and celebrations.

In general terms, the video homages that I will be referring to were elaborated from a series of photographs obtained from the internet showing different moments in the life of Cabral, whose trajectory is reconstructed at the scale of the everyday. This story is told by introducing textual fragments at the bottom of each image that complete the historical information about his life. Music plays a central role in these representations because it introduces, through its affective power and its lyrics, a set of themes familiar to any member of the Cape Verdean diaspora.[35] In this case, themes introduced in the songs are reinforced by the images, whose combination generates a visual discourse that articulates different representations.[36] The videos' intertextual montage enables a simultaneity of codes (visual, aural, and written) that constitute a powerful language.

The video I will discuss was projected forty years after the assassination of Cabral in the context of a commemorative ceremony at the Cape Verdean Society of Dock Sud. The video begins with a fragment of the documentary *Cabralista*[37] that introduces some images of the Cape Verdean leader and raises the subject of his assassination. This topic will be present during the length of the projection, since it evokes memories of the impact the news of Cabral's assassination had on the Cape Verdean Society in Argentina.[38] The video follows Cabral's life trajectory, juxtaposing photographs from his student years in Lisbon and his house in Cape Verde and texts that show his progressive political awareness until the organization of the PAIGC. As his development as leader is portrayed on screen, it is combined with the memories of his presence as related by Miriam Gomes[39] in a filmed interview incorporated into the video. The interview abandons an omniscient perspective and presents Gomes's narrative directly.[40] This reinforces the testimonial effect of her words and at the same time focuses attention on how these events were experienced in Buenos Aires. Gomes gives an account of what happened in the community before independence and she provides details about the tensions of this period.[41] As the video continues, and reaches its culmination with Cabral's assassination, Gomes reappears and relates the repercussions this event had on the Cape Verdean Society in Buenos Aires. In addition to stressing the highly negative effect of the assassination, the video, by means of Gomes's testimony, shows how the independence process could not be interrupted once it had begun. The video continues by combining images from the period of independence on the islands: the raising of the new flag, a parade of children and youth, and some fragments of Arístides Pereira's speech during the independence ceremony.[42]

The use of photographic montage, incorporating documents and images from the internet and integrating them with fragments from interviews recorded on video, and the musical emphases given to certain "climaxes" (such as Cabral's assassination and the arrival of independence) construct an imaginary trajectory of Cabral's life that connects Cape Verde to the Cape Verdean community in Argentina, all of whose stories are linked by the use of the techniques mentioned above.

To summarize, the photographic images about Cabral and the period of independence that are owned by families, institutions, and archives are being reorganized by means of digital technologies, whose format introduces these images as "historical evidence," adding different layers of complexity to memories of past events. At the same time, the video memorials are uploaded to social media or platforms such as *YouTube*, enabling their circulation in new channels and re-contextualizing their meaning in these spaces. By doing this, the history that is represented in these videos establishes a dialogue with unknown, although imagined, viewers who intervene in a debate centered on the story of Amílcar Cabral.

Conclusion

This essay tried to show the relations, mediations, and recognitions at play when digital media were incorporated into specific social contexts, a process that set in motion a significant interaction between the search for documentary information, the process of digitization, and the memories and representations they enable and that transform objects as they become documents.

In particular, I attempted to reconstruct different situations that use new technologies to represent the history and collective memory of Argentinian-Cape Verdeans. As I have pointed out, these activities revolve around the project of consolidating an Afrodescendant digital archive, whose digitized information calls attention to the complexity of Cape Verdean history and provides material for dynamic individual and collective self-representations. At the same time, these videos provide novel ways of remembering and develop explicative discourses that fine-tune and contextualize the classifications and organizational criteria of the documentary corpus, which is important because of the challenge in applying collective criteria to organize the information. Indeed, from the beginning the planning undertaken for the archival project has been accompanied by activities that seek to expose these documents in diverse contexts (memorials, documentary projections,[43] and photographic exhibitions). Because of this, these documents are re-signified and given new meanings, since they are linked to images in order to construct alternative visual discourses.

In the case of the videos I have analyzed, one can see how the use of resources such as images, documentary information made available through its digitization, and—more fundamentally—music permit the articulations of meaning with transnational youth from Cape Verde and Guinea-Bissau that re-create the process of "Africanization" experienced by contemporary Afro-Argentinian youth. This is achieved by creating new interpretations that reclaim Cabral's pan-Africanist legacy so as to re-signify it in the present context. Indeed, some of the speeches in these commemorations recover Cabral's call to "re-Africanize the spirits" or to "stop being second-class Portuguese and become first-class Africans," both of which strongly resonate in an institution that is in the midst of a long process of redefinition and seeks to incorporate the claims of other Afrodescendant collectives.[44] To this one must add the status as evidence of the photographs, documents on paper, and filmed interviews that are transformed into testimonies substantiating that these events did take place. The evidentiary status of these and other documents is not a minor issue: as I stated at the beginning, the so-called common sense and still-extant notion that there are no "Afro-Argentinians" can continue to downplay the presence of Afro-Argentinians even when they appear in photographs.[45]

To the redefinition of sense or meaning one must add the change that accompanies the process of digitization through which certain photographs from domestic contexts become documents by being placed in the new horizon of meanings embodied by the archive itself. From mere domestic images and images of the everyday, they are transformed into documents that give evidence to the historical and actual presence of African descendants in Argentina. Indeed, once digitized, numerous photographs and documents on paper are currently being transferred from personal settings and domains to more impersonal circuits. In this process of redistribution (by means of photographic exhibitions, pamphlets, web pages, and social media), representations are created that politicize certain demands by Afrodescendants.[46] For example, some digitized photographs in the archive were given to state agencies committed to making Afrodescendants more visible.[47] In that case, we asked ourselves, Which images should we send? What is being visualized? In response to these questions, we tried to select images that gave evidence of a dynamic collective history; therefore, we privileged photographs of people in social functions, celebrations, and everyday situations. On the other hand, I also attempted to show images that exemplified the process of miscegenation in the context of the neighborhoods[48] and photographs of women and youth, usually underrepresented in visual documentation. Although these photographs are not yet "circulating," their meaning will probably be transformed as they are dissociated from specific family histories and will come to represent generic "Afrodescendant families" persisting through time.

Notes

1. Cape Verde is an African archipelago located in the Atlantic Ocean, 450 kilometers (280 miles) off the coast of Senegal. It is composed of ten major islands and five minor ones. The Barlovento group is located toward the west and includes the islands of Santo Antão, São Vicente, Santa Luzia (uninhabited), São Nicolau, Sal, and Boa Vista. The Sotavento islands lie closer to the continent and include Maio, Santiago (the capital), Fogo, and Brava.

2. The term "documents" refers here to a large and heterogeneous set of materials that include written sources and institutional sources (associational acts and membership lists, personal documents, correspondence, newspapers, poetry, recipes, and photographs from both institutional and personal collections); theses written by researchers on topics related to Latin American Afrodescendants; and audiovisual archives (interviews with, or recordings about, institutional figures and activists), including videos, shorts, and documentaries made by current descendants of the Cape Verdean immigrants. It is important to clarify that, given the polysemy of the word "document," the range of archives and documentation can expand even further as we learn more about the digitization of information, the politics of diffusion, and the criteria for classifying the material. See Sansone, "Os dilemas da patrimonialização."

3. A Cape Verde policy of openness in 1990, which coincided with a period of parity between the US dollar and Argentinian peso, stimulated travel by descendants to the archipelago. This, in turn, increased awareness of the political and social reality on the islands.

4. Among others, see Andrews, *The Afro-Argentines*; Frigerio, "De la 'desaparición' de los negros"; and Geler, *Andares negros, caminos blancos*.

5. See Martino, "Reflexiones sobre imágenes fotográficas"; Geler, *Andares negros, caminos blancos*; and Maffia, *Desde Cabo Verde a la Argentina*.

6. *Mestizaje* (miscegenation) refers to processes of interbreeding, in biological, social, and cultural terms that have a permanent character; see Frigerio, "De la 'desaparición' de los negros." Florencia Guzmán observes how these processes generate changing cultural and collective affiliations (hybridization) according to the contexts of interaction and following a hierarchical logic in which differences are organized; see Guzmán, *Los claroscuros del mestizaje*.

7. See Sansone, "Os dilemas da patrimonialização."

8. Some of these topics have been addressed by Alejandro Frigerio (2008), Fernández Bravo (2013), Lea Geler (2016), and Martino (2016), among others.

9. Da Silva Catela, "Re-velar el horror," 3.

10. See Ardèvol, Stalella, and Domínguez, "Introducción."

11. See Ardèvol, Stalella, and Domínguez, eds, *La mediación tecnológica*; and Arriaga, "Representaciones, escalas e identidades afrodescendientes."

12. Hall, "La cultura," 222.

13. See Poole, *Visión, raza y modernidad*.

14. Characteristic of the oeuvre of Bruno Latour and Michel Callón, as noted in Ardèvol, Stalella, and Domínguez, eds, *La mediación tecnológica*, 12.

15. Ibid.

16. See Frigerio and Lamborghini, "Los afroargentinos."

17. Malinowski quoted in Quirós, "Etnografiar mundos vívidos," 50.

18. *Porteño* is a term that refers to the inhabitants of Buenos Aires.

19. See Caggiano, "Conservar el vacío."

20. See Geler, "Categorías raciales en Buenos Aires."

21. See Lévi-Strauss, *El pensamiento salvaje*.

22. There are currently different stances on whether to consider Cape Verdean descendants as Afro-Argentinians. Some reject it out of hand and argue that the term Afro-Argentinians defines those who descend from slaves (who arrived in the country against their will as part of the slave trade). Since Argentinian-Cape Verdeans arrived as immigrants, they would not qualify as Afro-Argentinians under this criterion. Such positions maintain essentialist classifications that are meant to be permanent. I, on the contrary, consider that, in spite of the significance of such a differentiation (and without rejecting those who live with it), the long temporal span of Cape Verdean immigration and a complex process of national incorporation and identity refinement merits their inclusion as Afro-Argentinians.

23. The activists who converged at the 2001 Durban conference against racism (South Africa) established a consensus on the use of the category "Afrodescendant," whose strategic use sought to emphasize descent over and above membership in a racial community. See Geler, *Andares negros, caminos blancos*.

24. The activists working together on projects since 2001 and who appeal to this category have experienced different forms of social insertion in Argentina. Because of this, the demands each of them make and the legitimate mechanisms to deal with their claims do not necessarily coincide. A heterogeneous set of social groups that includes slaves' descendants, people who have arrived in different periods from various Latin American countries, and even the most recent immigrants from Sub-Saharan Africa (1990) are defined at various times and places as "Afrodescendants." Other categories predating the 2001 Durban conference, such as "Afro-Argentinian," "Africans," "Afro," and "Afro-Argentinans from the colonial trunk" make a complex panorama of individual and collective affiliations that change in time and space.

25. See Fernández Bravo 2013, "¿Qué hacemos con los afrodescendientes?"; and Frigerio, "De la 'desaparición' de los negros."

26. Arriaga, "Representaciones, escalas e identidades afrodescendientes."

27. See Martino, "Afro/argentinos caboverdeanos en Buenos Aires."

28. Ibid.

29. Partido Africano da Independência da Guiné e Cabo Verde (African Party for the Independence of Guinea and Cape Verde) is a bi-national party that gave birth to political pan-Africanism.

30. Gomes, "Las comunidades negras en la Argentina."

31. Maffia, *Desde Cabo Verde a la Argentina*.

32. Because of its strategic location, the Cape Verde islands operated as a commercial transitional port in the capture and traffic of slaves sent to the Americas (Brazil).

33. Cape Verdeans arrived in Argentina at the end of the nineteenth century and the beginning of the twentieth century—during the Portugal colonization—with a steady decline in the number of immigrants until the 1960s; see Maffia, *Desde Cabo Verde a la Argentina*. Their settlements in coastal areas led them to organize their institutions around those locales. Some of the oldest Cape Verdean settlements in the world are in Argentina: the Cape Verdean Society of Ensenada (1927), the Society of Mutual Aid, and the "Cape Verdean Society of Dock Sud" mentioned earlier.

34. See Cabral, *Nacionalismo y cultura*.

35. Among these themes one finds some that recur time and again: relations that were interrupted when emigrating, and loves left behind on the islands, among others.

36. See Díaz Barrado, "Imágenes para la memoria."

37. The documentary *Cabralista* reconstructs the leader's revolutionary trajectory from the perspective of a younger generation of Cape Verdeans born post-independence.

38. The approach to this debate (who killed Cabral?) by Cape Verdeans of Argentina is dealt with in magazines that are in the process of being digitized. An issue of the magazine *Panorama Africano*, edited in Bernal (Buenos Aires, Argentina), was dedicated to this topic. These publications remained in storage for a long period because of the civilian-military dictatorship in Argentina (which coincided with the period in which Cape Verde achieved independence). The themes explored in this particular issue probably elicited many conflicts in the segments of the institution that identified as Portuguese.

39. Miriam Gomes is a first-generation Cape Verdean descendant and a renowned intellectual and activist advocating for the rights of Afro descendants in Argentina.

40. Guarini, "Los límites del conocimiento."

41. The recent digitization of the institutional decrees from this period (1960–1975) has made these conflicts better known.

42. Numerous photographs of this "break" in Cape Verde's history record the independence celebrations organized in the Argentinian capital. Currently, such images are beginning to be digitized and projected in memorials and events, redefining their importance during a period of apparent "non-existence" of Afrodescendants.

43. These were extremely interesting as inter-generational and inter-disciplinary dialogues. A roundtable, which followed the projection of the *Cabralista* documentary, included members of the Cape Verdean Society and anthropologists who have close links with the organization. The debate explored several thematic axes based on the projection of the photographs of activities in Buenos Aires during the period of the islands' independence. The projections took place in the Cape Verdean Association of Dock Sud and in cultural centers during the month of July, which is the month the independence of the islands is commemorated. More projections and movie showings are being planned. More information can be found on the following website: http://www.centrocultural.coop/modules/piCal/index.php?action=View&event_id=0000105329.

44. See Cabral, *Nacionalismo y cultura*.

45. See Fernández Bravo, "Fotografía y nación."

46. See Da Silva Catela, "Re-velar el horror."

47. The photographs were requested by INADI (National Institute against Discrimina-

tion, Xenophobia, and Racism) from some members of GEALA (Afro-Latin American Study Group) in the context of the celebration of the International Decade of Afrodescendants this past November 8.

48. There are numerous photographs of Argentinian-Cape Verdeans in the neighborhood of Dock Sud, some of whom circulate on the internet and help render a more complex view about the dynamics of race mixing among Afro-Argentinian families.

Bibliography

"Amílcar Cabral, La Lucha de Liberación desde Adentro." Produced by Patricia V. Gomes and Rogério Rocha and presented at Dock Sud on January 5, 2015, to mark the forty-second anniversary of Cabral's assassination. Video, 12:06. https://www.youtube.com/watch?v=hzNPcvrKryQ.

Andrews, George Reid. *The Afro-Argentines of Buenos Aires: 1800–1900*. Madison: University of Wisconsin Press, 1980.

Ardèvol, Elisenda, Adolfo Stalella, and Daniel Domínguez, eds. "Introducción: La mediación tecnológica en la práctica etnográfica." In *La mediación tecnológica en la práctica etnográfica*, 9–29. País Vasco: Ankulegi/Elkartea, 2008.

———. *La mediación tecnológica en la práctica etnográfica*. País Vasco: Ankulegi/Elkartea, 2008.

Arriaga, Eduard. "Representaciones, escalas e identidades afrodescendientes en la era digital: Búsquedas personales, proyectos globales e interconexión." *Journal: Afrolatinoproject. org*, 2013. https://edyarr.github.io/.

Cabral, Amílcar. *Nacionalismo y cultura*. Barcelona: Ediciones Bellaterra, 2013.

Cabralista, a documentary trilogy written and directed by Valerio Lópes, 2011, 56 minutes. https://www.youtube.com/watch?v=KJab5uePfyk.

Caggiano, Sergio. "Conservar el vacío: Imágenes de la desaparición de los negros en el Archivo General de la Nación." *Corpus, Archivos virtuales de la alteridad americana* 6, no. 2 (2016). https://doi.org/10.4000/corpusarchivos.1740.

Da Silva Catela, Ludmila. "Re-velar el horror: Fotografía, archivos y memoria frente a la desaparición de personas." In *Memorias, Historia y Derechos Humanos*, edited by Isabel Piper Shafir and Belén Rojas Silva. Santiago de Chile: Programa Domeyko Sociedad y Equidad, Universidad de Chile, 2012.

Díaz Barrado, Mario P. "Imágenes para la memoria: La fotografía en soporte digital, en Pasado y Memoria." *Revista de historia contemporánea* 3 (2004): 5–45.

Fernández Bravo, Nicolás. "¿Qué hacemos con los afrodescendientes? Aportes para una crítica de las políticas de la identidad." In *Cartografías afrolatinoamericanas: Perspectivas situadas para análisis transfronterizos*, edited by Florencia Guzmán and Lea Geler, 241–62. Buenos Aires: Biblos, 2013.

———. "Fotografía y nación: Reflexiones antropológicas sobre las fotografías con afroargentinos. *Corpus, Archivos virtuales de la alteridad americana* 6, no. 2 (2016). https://doi.org/10.4000/corpusarchivos.1746.

Frigerio, Alejandro. "De la 'desaparición' de los negros a la 'reaparición' de los afrodescendientes: Comprendiendo la política de las identidades negras, las clasificaciones raciales y de su estudio en la Argentina." In *Los estudios afroamericanos y africanos en América Latina:*

Herencia, presencia y visiones del otro, compiled by Gladys Lechini, 117–44. Buenos Aires: CLACSO, 2008.

Frigerio, Alejandro, and Lamborghini, Eva. "Los afroargentinos: Formas de comunalización, creación de identidades colectivas y resistencia cultural y política." In *Afrodescendientes y africanos en Argentina*, edited by Rubén Mercado and Gabriela Catterberg, 1–51. Buenos Aires: PNUD, 2011.

Geler, Lea. *Andares negros, caminos blancos: Afroporteños, Estado y Nación Argentina a fines del siglo XIX*. Rosario: Prohistoria, 2010.

———. "Categorías raciales en Buenos Aires: Negritud, blanquitud, afrodescendencia y mestizaje en la blanca ciudad capital." *Runa* 1 (2016): 71–87.

Gomes, Miriam. "Las comunidades negras en la Argentina: Estrategias de inserción y mecanismos de invisibilización." In *Afroargentinos hoy: Invisibilización, identidad y movilización social*, edited by Marta Maffia and Gladys Lechini. La Plata: Universidad Nacional de La Plata, 2009. https://alfarcolectivo.files.wordpress.com/2013/10/libro-final.pdf.

Gomes, Patricia V. Video produced to mark the fortieth anniversary of Cabral's assassination. Presented at Dock Sud, on January 20, 2013. https://www.youtube.com/watch?v=C-ek2RbRJx4.

Gomes, Patricia V., and Rogério Rocha. Video produced to mark the forty-second anniversary of Cabral's assassination. Presented at Dock Sud, on January 5, 2015. https://www.youtube.com/watch?v=hzNPcvrKryQ.

Guarini, Carmen. "Los límites del conocimiento: La entrevista fílmica." *Revista Chilena de Antropología Visual* 9 (June 2007): 1–12.

Guzmán, Florencia. *Los claroscuros del mestizaje: Negros, indios y castas en la Catamarca colonial*. Córdoba: Encuentro Grupo Editor, 2010.

Hall, Stuart. "La cultura, los medios de comunicación y el 'efecto ideológico.'" In *Sin garantías: Trayectorias y problemáticas en estudios culturales*, edited by Eduardo Restrepo, Catherine Walsh, and Víctor Vich, 221–54. Popayán: Envión Editores, 2010.

"Homenaje a Amílcar Cabral (A 40 años de su asesinato)." Produced by Patricia V. Gomes and presented at Dock Sud on January 20, 2013, to mark the fortieth anniversary of Cabral's assassination. Video, 18:06. https://www.youtube.com/watch?v=C-ek2RbRJx4.

Jelin, Elisabeth. "La fotografía en la investigación social: Algunas reflexiones personales." *Memoria y Sociedad* 16, no. 33 (2012): 55–67.

Lévi-Strauss, Claude. *El pensamiento salvaje*. México: Fondo de Cultura Económica, 1999.

Lópes, Valerio, dir. *Cabralista*, 2011. Bernin, France: MedeO Productions. https://www.youtube.com/watch?v=KJab5uePfyk.

Maffia, Marta M. *Desde Cabo Verde a la Argentina: Migración, parentesco y familia*. Buenos Aires: Biblos, 2010.

Martino, María Cecilia, "Afro/argentinos caboverdeanos en Buenos Aires: Procesos históricos, políticos e identitarios desde una perspectiva inter-generacional." PhD diss. Facultad de Filosofía y Letras, Universidad de Buenos Aires, 2015.

———. "Reflexiones sobre imágenes fotográficas, vínculos familiares e identidades entre argentinos/caboverdeanos de Buenos Aires." *Corpus, Archivos virtuales de la alteridad americana* 6, no. 2 (2016). https://doi.org/10.4000/corpusarchivos.1746.

Poole, Deborah. *Visión, raza y modernidad: Una economía visual del mundo andino en imágenes*. Lima: Sur, 2000.

Quirós, Julieta. "Etnografiar mundos vívidos: Desafíos de trabajo de campo, escritura y enseñanza en antropología." *Publicar* 12, no. 17 (2014): 47–65.

Rodrigues, Isabel F. "Islands of Sexuality: Theories and Histories of Creolization in Cape Verde." "Colonial Encounters between Africa and Portugal" special issue, *International Journal of African-Historical Studies* 36 (2003): 83–103.

Sansone, Livio. "Os dilemas da patrimonialização: Da invisibilidade á hipervisibilidade de alguns aspectos da cultura afro-brasileira." In *Cartografías afrolatinoamericanas: Perspectivas situadas para análisis transfronterizos*, edited by Florencia Guzmán and Lea Geler. Buenos Aires: Biblos, 2013.

9

Borrowing Digital Tools to Connect the Periphery

Interview with Alí Majul

EDUARD ARRIAGA AND ANDRÉS VILLAR

TRANSLATED BY EDUARD ARRIAGA AND ANDRÉS VILLAR

The editors engaged Alí Majul, an Afro-Colombian performance artist and activist, in discussions about his experience using digital technology in his artistic and activist practice. As one of the coordinators and most active members of Colectivo Contextos, a cultural collective in the Colombian city of Cartagena, Majul and his collaborators have created Canal Cultura [Culture Channel], a web presence that is used to disseminate information about alternative cultural events and activism, particularly in and for marginal communities, in the Americas and beyond. Majul proposes that a healthy critical wariness of the digital needs to be fostered in Afro-Latinx and peripheral communities at large.

This was a written interview that was performative in the sense that Majul's answers were as much actions as they were statements—for example, terms that in Spanish are gendered, such as *nosotros* and *nosotras* (translated as us, male and female, respectively) were written by Majul as *nosotrxs*, which like the term Latinx makes the gender indeterminate or open. Moreover, Majul's language is frequently allusive and poetic rather than merely descriptive. This also helps express his distrust of academic writing and knowledge and conveys Majul's allegiance to his community, neighborhood, city, and region.

* * *

1. What is the role of digital tools in your practice and in the development
of your work (in contrast with analog and more traditional tools)?

I feel that I have managed to depoliticize the fiction that is known as technology. A fiction of power, a late fiction that has created a geopolitics of
ignorance of our bodies. That damaging idea of development and technology kills me, annihilates me, ends me, diminishes me. I know that my body
is a digitized capitalization, a gore. In the place they occupy in my practices
these digital tools continue to be colonizing agents. I know and recognize
those privileges. With my resistance I rescue an ancestral and pedagogical
communitarian narrative immersed in an affective politics that seeks to decentralize such whitewashed [*blanqueadas*] and hegemonic practices. I have
always suggested looking for a more loving utopia within this misogynistic
and hetero-centric hyper-digitalization. I think that the most affective resistance to the digital and the traditional is to return to what is from the
neighborhood [*lo barrial*], to the communal, to the hills, to the village lane,
to the mountains, to what no one dares to talk about, and to what no one in
their living days has been able to imagine.

2. What attributes or characteristics of digital tools are the most useful
for you and your practice?

Something that has coincided with that power structure called technology is
the possibility of bringing together a swarm [*manada*] of artists, artivists, feminists, transfeminists, dissidents, and postcolonials from the South and the Caribbean, the Caribbean that I inhabit and it inhabits me. One of the characteristics [of digital tools] is that of bringing us together as a community of people
infected by rage, by unease, by this precarious world that lights us up and in
which we find ourselves; but we hurry to defend ourselves and take care of the
others. That is why we infect with our witchcraft from all digital platforms, the
bitch that we are, abortive, shaman-like, Indigenous, and forever Black. I would
not call my experience a job, although many would consider it that way. I call
it an exchange and a recognition of historically forgotten territories. Another
characteristic [of digital technology] is to generate tension, to blow your mind,
to stir a debate with all our fluids and all our shit with everyone I interview. It is
a matter of creating a constant becoming that does not let us feel and criticize
how we are. A becoming bitch that lets us express and transgress as we want.

3. What positive and negative effects does the digital have on your culture (local, regional, national, ethnic, etc.)?

Look, I feel that we all practice a pedagogy of cruelty, as Rita Segato would say.[1] A pedagogy of cruelty in both the digital and non-digital. We exert thousands of systematic oppressions, and some people choose to hide behind the label of activists, ending up articulating a semiotics of incoherence and an opportunistic, slick, and spineless critique. I feel that, in my experience, in the virtual I have impoverished the territory where I have developed my artistic and community proposals. I have also fallen into that perverse game of instrumentalizing the community. Not only me, but many others who are part of the same resistance, the same video, the same circuit. Another thing is that we want to make academic material of our experiences on social networks as if the academy were the best there is; but, no—it's not that way. We might be able to build nice spaces that are also political, but the academy will always be a white-colonial epistemic police. Actually, it really bothers me when we playact as intellectuals on Facebook or any other social network. That is a negative thing; it is shameful. In this respect I don't have a "dignified" or politically correct thing to say that will make me look good.

4. Do you think the digital helps communities identified or self-identified as belonging to the African diaspora connect or re-connect among themselves and with communities in Africa? If not, why?

The digital did not help to construct me or deconstruct me. The digital did not help me walk with my buddies in the communities where I radicalize my communitarian pedagogy. The digital led me to create a series of imaginaries of things that are almost never true. I had to build in the street, in Cartagena's Bazurto Market, in the shantytown, in buses, with whores [putas], with trans, with very crazy people. I love that. I had to do it in silence, in the racket, in the disorder, in cowardice, and almost never out of courage, although I always wanted to do it out of love. I came to know by walking and pounding the pavement, and I'm not sure if one can really help reconnect communities. I have always been roaming there. My true connection with Afro-Colombian communities is through intersectionality and the love that unites us. Love is the real revolution; nothing else.

5. Why do you think it is important to establish or preserve connections, particularly in the so-called "digital age," among these Afro-diasporic communities and between them and Africa?

I do not know if our priority as Afro-Caribbeans is to preserve digital connections. I rather think that they have screwed us and not in the idiotic fashion of re-victimizing ourselves. We're fed up with the way the distribution of goods in this country left us in the lurch, with a state that is increasingly necro-political, austere, deceitful, lying, and cruel. I feel that what endures and connects us is that. The rest will follow when they comply with our wishes.

6. What role does the nostalgic and the utopian play in the digital projects that seek to reconnect or make visible Afrodescendant cultural attributes?

As I said in the previous answer, all of this is nostalgic: that they do not comply with our wishes is nostalgic and criminal; that they are killing us socially is nostalgic. It is nostalgic that we are politicizing a war and that we are absorbing it in our bodies and our lives. We are bodies that do not count for the system; we are embodying racism in our own flesh; we are in a carceral system that does not let us breathe; we are dead and we have become accustomed to it to survive. What more? Utopian is to keep believing that our lives will be better and different; I've already lost hope in my work, in art, and in many other things. I am an ill person who likes to think of a global utopia and be very happy about all the learning that is kindled in our territories and communities. The way to go, guys [chicxs], is to continue on a war footing, in swarms; all of the results must be exhibited by using networks. We must show the world that we are not alone. It is important to accompany each other virtually in all these projects. We need to create a loving politics digitally that keeps us alive. I survive with The Route of the Women from the Periphery [La Ruta de las Mujeres de la Periferia] and with things that are said in Canal Cultura with a love for other processes that are being gestated in all of the South and the Caribbean. For example, The Route starts next month with the first Caribbean Communal Anti-Racist Feminist School [Escuela Feminista Antirracista Comunitaria Caribeña], and for me it is very beautiful to have such powerful people interested in the communal and peripheral. We will have Yuderkys, Astrid Liliana Angulo, Ashanti, Dorothy Carabalí and many more.[2] That reconnects me anew with that utopia, the utopia of feeling other experiences and other bodies in these territories, and of building a powerful Afro memory in the Colombian Caribbean, which in fact already exists and is powerful. But we need to fill our digital spaces with what we do and love. It will serve to overthrow so much hegemony of the right[3] that screws us.

7. Who is in charge of programming, design, hosting, and technical support for your projects? Are these local people or organizations from your community, or are they individuals from other places connected to more global servers and services?

Carlos [Castro] Macea is the person in charge of the programming of Canal Cultura. He is in charge of the design, of uploading the content I get by interviewing people and creating reports, and of technical support for the whole project. With Carlos we have generated something cool, which is to construct a communal memory by using film, journalism, documentaries, and activism. It is a dissident space in Cartagena and the whole region. Each time, Canal Cultura creates a space that has been won by the skin of our teeth. We have no budget, but we do everything with love and with an affective radicality of uniting the places where nothing arrives and there is nothing; we are concerned with giving everything to our territories. They read us in Mexico, Spain, Brazil, Chile, Ecuador, Colombia, Dominican Republic, Venezuela, Argentina, Bolivia, and places I cannot even imagine. Of course, these people taking part in The Route and Cartagena come from the street, they taste of the hills, they taste of periphery, they are smeared in mud; they are local agents. One doesn't need to know it—one knows that they are present in the struggles. They do not need an academic degree to prove they are people, that their work is strong, visceral, and committed. That is why I love the work realized by my colleagues Alex Cermeño, Leidy Chaverra, Darlys Bonfante, Adriana Molina, the people of Funsarep, and the work done by thousands of male and female leaders who accompany us in our mobilizations.[4]

8. What impact does the incorporation of those local or global actors have on the development of your projects?

You know, I admire greatly the work done by Cartagena's community mothers. I admire those who working with the Indigenous people of Menbrillal are fighting and resisting the crap that the system, the government, and the corrupt politicians of Cartagena are inflicting on them. I admire the popular and neighborhood-focused [*barrial*] work promoted by Funsarep, a work that serves everyone in the city. I admire young people in the municipalities, the countryside, and *corregimientos*[5] who are wagering on change, and not on that idea of change that this hyper-masculinist [*machirulo*] paramilitary neoliberal system wants to shove us into and sell us by force. I want to make it clear there are many possible bets for Cartagena in my inkwell that are brilliant, but I can't remember their names. The impact is great. But in response to your question, I dare to say that those male and female leaders that are in their neighborhoods are important, and they don't expect to showcase their work in the media. This tension of stressing the big figures has to be undone; it's the leaders whom nobody knows about as they work in silence. Their silence is caustic, their results implacable. Now, there are leaders who hide in that silence, which sometimes is violent, to commit a crime and to steal. That is not the question, it is the geopolitics of leaders we do not know about and who are more present than me in the local and community scene. Their work is necessary, it is vital. It's a web that must not get lost and shouldn't be diminished by other "authorized" voices that are used to speaking for everyone. Let's dismantle those privileges and the violence that do not allow us to talk and take action. Finally, everything that is local is a true bet for the city and for everything outside the city's machinery.

9. What type of infrastructure do you use to build your projects (taking into account that infrastructure can be defined not only in terms of computers and digital networks, but also in terms of all the structures needed to bring a project to fruition)?

Look, Eduard: one doesn't have a computer and such things, but one has a lot of eagerness. What we have is borrowed and we honor those loans. Thanks to that we can show movies, we can organize conferences, and we can do a lot of things that greatly help all our projects. We have people who are always willing to live this experience. The community is the most important thing, and also the male and female leaders. I am sure that without all of this nothing of what I have described in the previous questions would become a reality.

10. When you design your digital projects do you take into account connections between software, hardware, work, and material resources? Why?

I'll be honest: I know nothing about that. I always ask or find out from people with strengths in those topics. I realize I should know about this because of my experience and because of what I do every day. But I've fallen asleep, I've cooled down even though I know there are people who have dedicated their whole life [to that]. It is really Carlos Castro Macea who advises me and helps me with all the digital design and with the resources necessary for what we want to achieve.

11. What do you see as the benefits or drawbacks of the term "Afro-digital," particularly when you reflect on your own practice?

I didn't know about that tension generated from the racial and the technological. To put it differently: I know it exists, but not in these scenarios. I think I play the fool with respect to various discussions. I personally think that the Afro must set fire to the digital, it must penetrate it, it must touch it, it must flood it; there is a real possibility there for legitimating spaces that historically have been denied to us. That negation must become an abolition; we can no longer keep perpetuating that they hide us; let's transit through those spaces of power where white people have been. We can't permit that in our projects, our struggles, and our fights—which have not been easily won—it is the white people who narrate it for us. But I'm sure that it's important to be conscious of who represents us as an Afro community, who are our Afro leaders, who speaks for us as Afro; in short, we should be very careful. Not everything recognized as Afro is part of our struggle and wants to be a part of it. As a consequence of this last issue, I wouldn't park myself in the Afro: my feeling and my rebelliousness accompanies the Indigenous, the Caribbean, the peasant farmers, and other struggles that have been ignored. I won't speak of benefits and inconveniences, but I do opt for an intersectional struggle. We must bring to the digital—and not only to the digital—those narratives that almost nobody knows about; create counter-narratives proceeding from language, from the visual, from the street, from what is known as aesthetics, from the TV, from all the places of power.

12. Afro-digital connections suggests an expansive terrain of possibilities that perhaps could not be achieved otherwise. What are the challenges in establishing such digital connections? What cultural elements could be created, renovated, or strengthened by the effects of digital connections on your field of action and on the Afrodescendant world in particular?

That is a complex question; I don't know if I can answer it. I'll risk speaking what I feel, given the little experience I have, and without hurting anyone. The real challenge begins by challenging the academy, by challenging the para-military-state, the narco-state that governs us; by challenging the tough guys who have always killed us and go on killing us. The challenge is to initiate a space with the community, a dialogue; it's to sit down to listen to them; it's to stop colonizing the community and the periphery as a spectacle. Better yet, to decolonize so many things. It's learning from the other; it's giving up oneself in body and with all the senses to the territory; it's being affected again with the other. I know I haven't said anything different in my answers; it's a con-stant repetition. It's a performance of unburdening for me. That unburdening needs to be incited in our spaces; it's necessary to speak, it's necessary to de-institutionalize so as not to intimidate. We frighten, and in many instances we are guilty and responsible for the fact that our communities do not talk to us. It's necessary to get closer, to heal ourselves, to love each other, to take care of each other for what is coming. I like to turn to our past and our present, to turn to the games of our youth and establish a line of the digital there, explaining ev-erything step by step. I feel that reading-theater [*lecto-teatro*] would very much help to heal us and learn things we don't know, and it's propitious that we all learn. Video tutorials, meetings in our houses, meetings with our grandfathers and grandmothers as Afro referents to help us create space for identity, and for an encounter with the digital and our memory.

13. "Digital humanities" is a concept that has become widely adopted in particular geographical regions. From your perspective, which of your project's elements could be included in the field of the digital humanities? If you have not heard of the concept, you can discuss the conception of the human and its connection to the digital in your projects.

Look, I find it difficult to discuss the human in a panorama in which it has been very easy to de-humanize. It's like when they ask me if I'm a feminist; my answer is "no." It's a "no"; I'm not careful, I don't take care of others as I should, I'm not affective, I'm egotistical. Despite my wagers and experiences of being a radical affectivity, I feel there are things I haven't healed. I can't be a feminist nor even less an activist, and less a human when my mother is sick in bed, or when my mother has to literally grind her body working as a domestic servant. Meanwhile, I speak in an auditorium of "more important things"; this doesn't make sense. The task it to create networked chains of global care. In the digital this must be political in its care, and it should gestate help for the people who need it. From the digital, to listen to and help thousands of migrants in Europe and the United States being driven to oblivion. Initiate cooperative networks for our Sierra Leone sisters and brothers; in short, so many things that must be said and denounced in networks, and we do nothing.

14. How much do your projects contribute to the creation of knowledge or the process of rethinking what we consider knowledge?

You know—I don't worry about that; but my preoccupations are rooted in re-thinking ourselves among ourselves. In questioning ourselves and interpellating ourselves as a community. One day I met a woman from a *corregimiento* in Cartagena during one of the workshops by The Route of the Women from the Periphery. She had been abused when she attended the workshop, and her partner already had a criminal record. She couldn't make the decision to end her situation. The workshop leader continuously interpellated the group of women, and she was of course also questioned. They formed a cartography of the territory, and the workshop was successful in helping them to speak and express themselves. It was painful to listen to many of the stories; the workshop ended. After a month, I met a woman who acted as a mediator during the session. She told me that this other woman had left her partner. I found that gratifying; I know one's contribution is a very small speck. But I like this more; it makes me happy. I think that this is my reason for being; I'm not concerned with the issue of the production of knowledge. It's something that I am conscious of, but this changes many things in our experiences.

15. In your view, what is the role of digital tools in making visible and overcoming racism, gender discrimination in all its forms, and other types of discrimination?

It is critically important, Eduard. I feel that we must create technological bombs. Bombs with which we paralyze everything. It's important to create digital cartographies that help us take care of each other. It's important to create points in networks where we can socialize and take action about the racism we live from day to day. It's important to generate dialogues with the media from within the networks, and to confront them; like a broken record, we must repeat when they kill a buddy who is trans, when there is a femicide, when they kill social leaders, when there is an expression of xenophobia or any other type of violation.

16. Given that the digital is extending to almost all corners of our lives, the potential audience for someone working in the digital realm is also increasing and becoming more diverse. With this in mind, to what audiences are your digital projects directed?

Look, I love all types of audiences. I feel that a seed is sown and that it grows, and grows with something inside it. That's the beauty when they ask, when there is that generation that from a young age motivates you to bring movies, or they look for you to tell you things that happen in their communities; and most importantly, when they themselves establish their own cultural spaces, artistic spaces, and of other types of spaces for the inhabitants there. Digital projects must be constructed with much care and love; each audience has something very special that differentiates it from other audiences.

17. In your opinion, in what ways has language, identity, race, ethnic affiliation, etc., been affected by the digital? How is this made evident in your projects?

In many ways. Note that there are many language communities that the digital ignores. But in a sense it's better this way. I feel that the digital also capitalizes, and that's not the idea. It converts the ancestral into something very hyper-consumerist, it deteriorates it, it squeezes the life out of it. It instrumentalizes it; this is also macabre; it's a systematic violence. It happens with issues of identity, it happens with race, it happens to things to which it should never happen. In my projects something happens, and it is that if I don't show them as digital, I can't find sponsors. That's cruel, it's tiring, it generates a pain in my body, it makes me sick. But that's how this is: a business with the look of a market. Better yet, whoever doesn't show doesn't sell. That's capitalism, brother. But what can I do? Do I stop pursuing my projects? Can someone show me another way? What do you suggest?

18. What is the conception (or conceptions) of the human that resides at the core of your artistic, technological, and social practice? In other words, what kind of human are you trying to address and represent by using digital media and digital tools?

Everyone; but there are still many restrictions. My mother is the answer. My mother doesn't yet know much about my experience and my investment with the community. She doesn't know about it because she doesn't have Facebook or any such social network. She doesn't have the time. She has her priorities and things that, like every Colombian woman in Cartagena, she has to resolve before sitting down to look at a phone or computer screen. Things must be made easier; one must generate content that is in no way academic. I like to talk with everyone. Our challenge and struggle is with everyone; if not, it's not a revolution.

19. What gave rise to Canal Cultura, The Route of the Women from the Periphery of Cartagena, and other related projects? What do you hope to achieve with these and similar initiatives, and what is their projection?

I'll speak about The Route of the Women from the Periphery. I got tired of falling asleep in my house without doing anything about the trans-femicides and femicides in all of the South and in the Caribbean. A dangerous plan of modernity was installed, frightening, blood-thirsty, that generates death and more death. On the other hand, I got tired that everything happened in an ableist [capacitista] center, a colonial center such as is Cartagena: binarist, heterosexual, white, and privileged. The Route arrives to have an impact from the space of community, from the neighborhood, from the popular, from where I have mentioned earlier; places where the academy doesn't go, where the academy and activisms fall short. I want to meet in the streets, and be told that they are generating their own resistances in their communities; that would make me happy. I would like it if they all construct networks together. Many times we live on the same street but know nothing about our neighbors, who they are and where they come from. Coming close to each other, talking with all of them is something political that we want to achieve, to initiate. That is a future project that I hope will be successful.

20. What other digital projects are you working on or are planning for the future?

At the moment, only on The Route. I'm working on a trans-media documentary about lesbians, and trans women and men in prison. That's where I'm at.

Notes

1. Rita Laura Segato is a Brazilian-Argentinian anthropologist. She has written extensively on gender violence.
2. Afro-Latinx artists, activists, and scholars.
3. Political right-wing forces.
4. Funsarep is a non-profit association founded in 1987 to defend the civil and human rights of Afrodescendants in Cartagena and the surrounding region. https://funsarep.org/.
5. A *corregimiento* is a municipal sub-unit created for administrative purposes to facilitate citizen participation and the delivery of public services.

10

Using Games to Build Connections in Africa and Beyond

Interview with Adebayo Adegbembo

EDUARD ARRIAGA AND ANDRÉS VILLAR

Adebayo Adegbembo is a Nigerian software developer and the founder of Genii Games (http://www.geniigames.com/), a software company that uses digital technologies to promote African culture. Adegbembo is featured here because his interview raises issues about the importance of digital technologies for creating connections across the African diaspora. His encounter with other Afrodescendants—for example, in Brazil—has made him aware of differences and commonalities across the diaspora. The issues Adegbembo raises in the interview resonate with the ones about transnational Blackness and the digitization of knowledge that have emerged in the other essays and interviews.

* * *

1. Where do digital tools fit into your media toolbox (in contrast to analog or more traditional media)?

For me, digital tools provide platforms for development, distribution, and engagement. More specifically, I use digital tools to plan, develop, publish, and engage with my audience. During transit, I use Evernote for drafting ideas for products or related articles. I also use tools like Adobe Illustrator to develop visuals to support my ideas. For development, I use a number of software, including Unity 3D, Adobe Flash Professional, and Xcode. Engagement involves the popular social media apps: Facebook and Twitter. Their ease of use ensures I have most at my disposal on a single device such as my phone or PC. Traditionally, pen and paper still come in handy, as I love sketching. In fact, I always have a writing pad and pencil with me.

2. What attributes or characteristics of digital tools are the most useful for you and your practice?

For development, scalability is important. I like to see that I can easily develop products for multiple platforms using one tool. I also like to see a good support system in terms of communities and resources devoted to such tools. That way, I can easily find help when I run into issues. I also like digital tools which support free or flexible pricing options with limited features. That way I can work without worries within the legal confines of what I can afford. Another useful attribute of digital tools, especially for distribution, is data-related support. By that I mean analytics that provide detailed information on users, such as their locations, use patterns, etc.

3. What are the positive and/or negative effects of the digital on your culture (national, regional, ethnic)?

Positives:

Ease of reach worldwide.

Ease of measurements and engagement.

Ease of creating awareness about cultural subjects.

Ease of content gathering, documentation, and preservation.

Negatives:

Low penetration of sophisticated digital tools such as Smartphones, especially within the rural space.

4. How does the digital help to connect, or re-connect, the African continent with the diasporas? Why do you think establishing or maintaining such connections is important in the so-called digital age? What role do the nostalgic and the utopian play in these kinds of projects?

Digital tools allow for the easiest means to reach and connect with the audience in ways that I couldn't even fathom in their absence. The obvious one is that the barrier to accessing data is now so low that one can plan, reach, engage, and even measure the degree of engagement. There's also a virtual bridge which connects the African continent and the diaspora vis-à-vis social media, global content distribution platforms, etc. Interestingly, the digital also fosters physical interactions aided by digital tools that initiate the process. The importance of these connections is necessary to further ensure alignment, and to spread learning and awareness about the core subject of our shared cultural identity.

Our history is deep with such traits as the transatlantic slave trade, and hence there's a sense of nostalgia when one sees that age-long traditions are shared across the world. That sense of nostalgia whets the appetite of people of African roots in their search for self-discovery and identity that is crucial to our being.

5. Who programs, designs, hosts, and provides technical support for your project? Are these various actors local, or are they connected to more widespread, even global, servers and services? What impact do you think this has, if any, on the nature of digital projects such as yours?

From a content development angle, our designers and programmers are local. We do, however, draw inspiration from concepts that are available globally. Our production tools are foreign, and hosting is done on foreign servers. Facebook is crucial in terms of analytics and engagement. In a nutshell, it's not a process in isolation when one considers the broader angles of engagement, distribution, and marketing alongside the fact that our audience is global. The impact is one that cuts across the global space, making it interesting.

6. What kind of infrastructure do you use in carrying out your project (considering that infrastructure could be defined not only as the computers and digital networks we use but all the structures involved in the execution of a project to make it happen)? Do you ever consider the connections between software, hardware, labor, and material resources when you think about, or design, your digital projects?

Considering the nature of our products and work, infrastructures in broader structural terms would include humans (teachers, voiceover artists), locations (recording studios), etc.

Yes, the planning phase usually involves making as many connections as possible. I personally relish the process of making the human, material, and cultural connections, and hence the basis of my background stories for the products created. There's also the end user, so one also looks at digital accessibility, language, and geographic considerations during the planning phase. In general, making these broader connections helps to see the process not in isolation but as connected. That's what makes the software and applications we produce relatable to people.

7. What benefits and/or drawbacks do you see in the terms such as "Afro-Digital," particularly if you reflect on your own practice?

The term Afro-Digital conjures the image of connectivity among people of African descent using technology across the world. From creation and distribution to engagement, the term captures the role that technology plays in promoting our common African identity. Within that context, it's beneficial in providing a bridge between our shared traits. It's also beneficial as a driver toward identifying with our rich history and culture. Additionally, it's beneficial in providing accurate contexts upon which to examine ourselves—our color, mother Africa, our religious beliefs, our languages, our manner of dressing, etc. In terms of drawbacks, it highlights the negative perceptions that we see in our divisions and lack of common empathy toward issues affecting every African regardless of location.

8. This book is about Afro-Latinx digital connections, although thinking in terms of Afro-digital connections more broadly across the African diaspora suggests an expansive terrain of possibilities that perhaps could not be achieved otherwise. What are some of the challenges in establishing such digital connections (whatever this may mean), and what could these connections create, renew, or reinforce? Has any connection with Afrodescendants in the Americas had an impact on your practice?

First and foremost, in some cases it's hard to get a sense of what African cultures mean to people outside Africa who do not have firsthand experience of the continent. Thankfully, that challenge is mitigated by the availability of digital tools. That availability creates possibilities for awareness, enlightenment, education, dissemination, and engagement with African cultures. That shared connection opens up to possibilities and vice-versa. In my opinion, a challenge is that there's still not a perfect capture of firsthand experiences that can only be promoted by physical human interactions. For example, with all the prior knowledge gained from reading about the influence of African cultures on Brazilians, this information could not compare with my firsthand experience of Brazil and its people, and with hearing from them what it takes to be Afro-Brazilian. Thus, while access to technology paved the way for us to find ourselves, nothing could be compared to the gains of physical interaction when we met in person. I think more of that needs to happen. There need to be more human interactions beyond what the digital allows. So while the digital will initiate these connections and conversations, physical interactions via exchange programs, live conferences, etc., will deepen them and reinforce the underlying message or subject.

9. We met in a conference whose main topic was the digital humanities. How do you think your project fits the digital humanities as a field? Has your conception of digital humanities changed after participating in that conference? What role do your projects play in contributing to knowledge or in helping us re-think what we consider knowledge?

Interestingly, the conference provided a structure to the subject, deepening how I understood the connection between the digital and humanities from an academic point of view. With that renewed understanding of the theoretical and academic perspectives, my project speaks more to the connection between the digital and humans. It solidifies the human angle which can seem missing. It reinforces the fact that behind analytics such as product downloads there are real humans who connect with the product's features and subjects in ways that serve a need. It's kind of personalized.

What we consider as knowledge is largely a result of what we know, which in itself is a product of what we consume. When it comes to Africa and its cultures, there's a historical trend of negative perceptions, so much so that there's an alarming effect on how Africans themselves perceive these things. Yet nowhere is a person complete in their understanding of themselves without coming to terms with their roots. I believe that much of these negative trends stem from different contexts that need to be brought to light. What projects like Genii Games Yoruba101 app do is bring these subjects to the fore within playful contexts in ways that stimulate interests in seeking more knowledge. They can motivate people to know more about their true identities, and promote conversations and engagement that are stepping-stones to seeking knowledge. Lastly, they reinforce the need to share more narratives about our experiences around our cultures. These can all become the basis for further research and knowledge sharing.

10. As the digital extends into virtually all areas of our lives, the potential audiences for anyone working digitally are, in theory, continually expanding. What is your project's intended audience, and how will digital tools help you connect to that audience?

Our intended audience is global, primarily kids with African roots. Secondarily, it's kids regardless of origin. The rationale for embracing both is to educate and entertain within the context of Africa's rich heritage. That's one way to counter negative perceptions in the secondary audience. For the primary audience, the main goal is to increase their connection, understanding, and confidence in their true self, from a cultural perspective.

Digital tools serve to continuously help us build, spread, and engage with individuals and organizations with whom we share values about promoting and preserving our Indigenous cultures. With the potential of these digital tools comes the push to be more creative, and also the push to leverage them for reach and engagement. We hope to innovate along those lines for effective and efficient ways of growing to meet our goals. In the end, the more sophisticated these tools, the better they are for our larger goal of using technology to promote and preserve our native cultures.

11. How do you see constructions such as language, identity and ethnic affiliation being affected by the power of digital technology? How do you address those changes in your practice?

From my experience, the influence that digital technology has over language is positive. It's what allows for engagement beyond physical borders. For example, I recently visited a popular Lagos market dominated by the Igbo-speaking people to engage with them about the diversity of their language and culture using the Igbo101 app as reference. In that instance, this app served a useful basis for driving conversation around the subject of their dialects, with consequent lessons which I'll be sharing in a coming article. Also, change by way of language variations or cultural appropriation is one that I consciously view positively, given such change raises awareness about the root cultures or languages in question. At Yale University's African language conference in October 2016, part of what I observed about the emerging trend of African languages among the youth is that digital tools provide ways to study, track, and evaluate how the languages are used or approached. In my practice, I try to be aware about the conversations, spotting influences and documenting them as much as I can. My goal is to use them as potential triggers in my apps, especially where they reflect trends in the audience. This is because our goals promoting native languages cannot be seen apart from societal trends such as language mixing and slang that in some cases is spurred by media technology. It is important to be aware of trends and other factors that the audience finds appealing. There always has to be a balance of play, fun, and learning in ways that the audience can relate to.

12. What conception(s) of humanity resides at the core of your artistic/ technological practice? In other words, what type of human being are you trying to both address and represent by using digital media and digital tools for language learning?

Our primary target is the child of African heritage, both inside and outside the African continent. Essentially, we seek to make these kids aware of their roots in a way that makes them self-confident and proud to be connected to its complex history and culture. We seek to give context even to the negative perceptions that Blacks often find stigmatizing about their roots. For example, I want my nieces, a five- and one-year-old, to grow into adults with a full sense of pride in their African cultural values such as languages. They should be confident to express themselves without fear or shame anywhere in the world. They should not have to wait for others to define who they are, or to buy into single narratives about their culture of origin.

13. How did the ideas for Igbo101 and other applications come about? What do you expect to achieve through programming these kinds of apps?

The idea for Igbo101, among other apps, was driven by the need to stimulate my niece and young neighbors to be interested in native cultural values. Delivering cultural subjects by leveraging what they already find appealing in foreign media means they can place the local and foreign on a par with one another. In other words, this helps them see that there is richness and value in their own Indigenous cultures.

14. What other digital projects are you working on?

At the moment we are working on subsequent versions of the existing apps. We are also working on a uniform structure to ease the delivery, across multiple mediums, of products covering various aspects of our diverse African cultures.

11

Epilogue

Using Digital Tools to Build Afro-Latinx Connections and Futures

EDUARD ARRIAGA AND ANDRÉS VILLAR

The chapters and interviews in this book elicit important issues about Afro-Latin American Blackness and Afro-Latinx digital connections that suggest three theoretical approaches current in the humanities and social sciences: decolonization, intersectionality, and posthumanism. These approaches have as many variations as there are practitioners, but a broad description of each is useful here. The call for decolonization arises from a rationale that sees colonial structures and hierarchies persisting into the present, even decades or centuries after former colonial territories achieve independence. A thorough decolonialization therefore requires more than a mere postcolonial condition: voices from the margins must be emphasized, rather than ones from normative centers that have been reproducing the colonial matrix with epistemological standards meant to "educate," "improve," and "develop" subaltern populations.[1] Intersectionality acknowledges the complexity of identities that cannot be subsumed or exhausted by one overarching category such as race. As the label suggests, identities are conformed by a manifold of intersecting issues such as class, gender, sexuality, and ability, among others, all of which must be addressed concurrently to deal effectively with the root causes of continuing injustice and oppression.[2] Lastly, the wide range of theories that can be subsumed under the rubric of posthumanism share a censure of anthropocentric knowledge and suggest that non-human life and objects are agents in their own right and should to be included in research about human concerns.[3] It is no surprise that these three approaches are linked, since at their core they advocate for a decentering of power, gender, and human mastery, which implies leaving behind the monolithic Man-as-Human we have inherited from the Enlightenment as we move toward a human pluralism that embraces multiplicity and difference.[4]

The conjunction of decolonization, intersectionality, and posthumanism might seem to be of interest only to academics, but as the examples in this book show, these three interlinked notions provide both a useful conceptual mesh that maps Afro-Latinx practices and a mutual validation to what is happening in academia and on the ground, so to speak: a deconstruction of Blackness, whose origin lies in the consecration of "race" as a system of classification and whose subsequent reconstitution increasingly refers to a global affinity attuned to distinct, regional expressions of Afrodescendant cultures.

It is important to keep in mind that all of this multiplicity and difference does not necessarily entail fragmentation. This is a crucial point that emerges quite clearly in the essays and interviews throughout the book. Afro-Latinx digital connections have emerged from the variegated possibilities and complexities of Afrodescendant identities, and at the same time digital connections have facilitated encounters and exchanges between the individuals and groups that cultivate these identities. As in other areas of life, digital tools provide a wide array of possibilities for presentation and self-representation, including for the expression of Blackness.

The notion of Blackness itself, however, is not as self-evident as it might seem. Michelle M. Wright has argued persuasively for an approach that locates it both in the current of history and in the lived present that constitute particular instantiations of individual and community identity.[5] An important consequence of such an approach is that it avoids the danger of reading Blackness too narrowly as a linear historical narrative originating only in the Middle Passage, an interpretation that has led to instances in which post-slavery arrivals from Africa have been rejected as not really being Black.[6] A horizontal or "rhizomatic" approach, suggests Wright, would more accurately describe the wide variety of Afrodescendant histories, demonstrating that "'Blackness' does not exist outside its intersection with other collective identities."[7] The unity in multiplicity inherent in Wright's notion of Blackness could be understood as an expansive consciousness, to adapt W. E. B. Du Bois's term into a positive force for Afrodescendant agency. Such consciousness, whose phenomenology includes the entanglement of analog and digital domains, is a flexible foundation for global and local alliances and mirrors other connections being built or fortified with the aid of digital technologies. It is a consciousness for the twenty-first century.

All of this ties in with much research about digital technologies and digital cultures that, proliferating across the globe, have established what Manuel Castells calls the "network society."[8] It is important to understand, Castells notes, that the internet and mobile technologies have opened up a space of hybridity in which individuation and autonomy can thrive, whereby individuation refers to the full expression of an individual's potential, and autonomy denotes a community's ability to challenge normative power when it becomes oppressive.[9] The internet, and the technologies linked to it, continues to provide the cyber-space and cyber-time that stimulate individuation and autonomy, despite the increasing colonization of the digital domain by conglomerates such as *Google*, *Facebook*, Apple, and the like. In particular, the internet and mobile technologies continue to be critical tools for social movements and identities in the Global South that are conditioned by the same dynamic we have ascribed to Blackness: the interplay of histories and lived experiences. This interplay generates Afro-Latinx digital connections as spaces of agency and modularity in which Black communities in the Americas innovate, propose alternative models of existence, and share experiences with other communities of the African diaspora.

The essays and interviews in this book show that digital technologies not only open new horizons for interacting and producing knowledge but they can also carry forward traits inherited from oppressive systems. Black communities have understood this paradox and so they continue to claim their agency in redesigning the world by challenging oppressive tendencies inherent in technological structures. Throughout history, many types of machines have been designed and programmed to annihilate Black communities and make them disappear, but it is thanks to communities' maroon connections and resourceful intersections that they continue to create digital and analog solidarities, retaining agency by having become, to use Jessica Marie Johnson's term, "deathless."[10]

Institutional vs. Community Knowledge

Intrinsic to Afro-Latin America and the development of Afro-Latinx connections is how history and lived experience affect the nature of knowledge: What is "valid" knowledge? What knowledge is important for individuals and communities to preserve? How can digital technologies help communicate such knowledge across a network of interested parties? How are digital technologies affecting epistemologies built in Afro-Latin America throughout the centuries? These questions are framed by what is an ongoing tension between institutional and community knowledge, a tension with important consequences for the creation and distribution of knowledge and that in this book acquires form in the contrast between the essays and the interviews.

The essays collected here are representative of institutional knowledge, and particularly of a broadly interpreted digital humanities, a field that has been promoted with much fanfare in the academy.[11] There are many facets in which the digital humanities intersect with what is happening in other academic domains such as anthropology, sociology, and communication studies, and as the digital humanities have grown, cross-fertilization has contributed productively to these conversations. Digital humanists, however, must be careful not to assume that there is only one type of digital humanities or that the digital humanities are immune from biases that have historically permeated the traditional humanities and society at large.[12]

Criticism from the humanities and social sciences has been quick to highlight the cultural and social frameworks in which technology is used and has given rise to movements such as the Black digital humanities, postcolonial digital humanities, decolonial computing, and digital posthumanities.[13] Emerging practitioners in Latin America and other parts of the world are also calling for a digital humanities that comprises traditions from different regions of the globe and stimulates a more democratic intercultural scholarly engagement.[14]

The research agendas described above seek to change the geopolitics of knowledge at the level of higher education, and it is undoubtedly the case that this is an important concern across Latin America—and particularly Afro-Latin America—where indices of inequality are high and access to even the most basic education is unevenly distributed. However, as the scenarios encountered in the essays and interviews make clear, it is in the domain of "informal" practices that Afro-Latinx digital connections and the assertion of Afrodescendant identities are ultimately grounded. Some of the major battles in Afro-Latin America against "epistemicide" are fought in the streets rather than in the halls of academia. In everyday life the possibilities for participating in the digital domain are numerous and not without danger, and digital interventions are attuned to local conditions, either by choice or by necessity.

Afro-Latinx Digital Praxis

One of the notable things about the texts collected here is how much the internet features throughout. The internet's reach is global, and it is therefore not surprising that it is an important tool used by Afrodescendants and other groups to disseminate information and build alliances. Additionally, the instantaneity of connections permits rapid criticism of racist events, online or offline, and the promotion of solidarity across international borders, as Mónica Carrillo notes in her interview.[15] This is of crucial importance for organizations such as *Afroféminas*, as seen in the interview with Sandra Abd'Allah-Álvarez Ramírez and in Maya Anderson-González's examination of Cuban bloggers, and for organizations that want to establish a presence on the internet, as Yvonne Captain demonstrates in her essay about Afro-Latin organizations online. These projects mirror others in different parts of the world, such as in Spain and Portugal, the former colonial masters of Latin America, where Afrodescendant individuals and communities are also taking advantage of the internet to counter their invisibility in the mainstream media.[16]

It is difficult to downplay the issue of invisibility that Afrodescendants have been subjected to and continue to endure in Latin America. The recognition of Afrodescendant identities was a major achievement that began with constitutional reforms in different countries of the Americas, but it has been difficult to apply much of the spirit of such reforms into practices and projects that change the everyday circumstances of poverty, inequality, and the lack of full rights of citizenship that persist in much of Latin America.[17] The inability or lack of will shown by governments across the continent to address structural problems that beleaguer most of Afro-Latin America makes it critical for non-governmental organizations to mediate between Afrodescendants and the state. Organizations such as CNOA or PretaLab do so by creating or fortifying links immanent to the communities they serve, links that are extended in space and time with the aid of digital tools.

In all of the examples collected here, expanded notions of Blackness underlie the digital strategies. Operations such as the "toolbox" mentioned in Eduard Arriaga's chapter take advantage of community links to provide access to digital technologies, and in such cases, human beings and their potentialities are an important element of the digital infrastructure, as is also noted by Alí Majul in his interview. This strengthens the suggestion that in our contemporary world, digital and analog relations are crucial for understanding Blackness in Afro-Latin America and elsewhere. Moreover, the examples highlighted throughout this book demonstrate that the digital is effective when it connects to local traditions to forge what this book has called Afro-Latinx digital connections.

It is also important to keep in mind that the idea of access to the possibilities inherent in digital technologies is informed by a history of social movements in Latin America and particularly to the philosophy of liberation and the pedagogy of Paulo Freire. This is another facet of the continuity between social movements that preceded the arrival of digital technologies and the wide variety of initiatives current today. Freire's approach to education is particularly relevant in terms of broadening the notions of epistemology, as Silvana Bahia notes in her reference to his book *Pedagogia da autonomia* (Pedagogy of freedom). In that book Freire reiterates his view of education as the means to promote what Manuel Castells defines as individuation and autonomy. Using a phrase made famous by Frantz Fanon, Freire called his lifelong work as pedagogy from the perspective of the "wretched of the earth," a project that PretaLab is also pursuing by combining digital and analog components that validate epistemology from the margins.[18]

The case study of the Cape Verdean archive examined by María Cecilia Martino is an interesting counter-example to Blackness defined solely in terms of slavery and the Middle Passage. The Cape Verdean community is the result of a modern wave of immigration to Argentina, and the histories collected by the archive seek to portray the contribution of this particular community's collective identity, which continues to retain ties with the "mother country." The problem here is a struggle against a double colonialism: an "internal" one in Argentina that, inherited from Spain, has ingrained a colonial matrix of racial difference into social structures; and a second one from Cape Verdean history, which is being retold through the documents being made available in the burgeoning archive. At stake is the decolonization of an Argentinian history that has subdued or ignored contributions by its Black citizens and the simultaneous retelling of Cape Verdean history, over which emigrants also have a claim. This project is an example of how grassroots movements can fill an institutional vacuum and create the conditions for advancing marginal histories not covered by the state. Importantly, the notions of Blackness built with video homages, documents, and stories are founded on transnational connections meant to strengthen local identities and bonds. This is a practical approach to the African diaspora that gives credence to Michelle M. Wright's assertion that categorical notions of Blackness need to be informed by the particularities of local histories and lived experiences.

The last interview in the book, with Adebayo Adegbembo, takes us outside Afro-Latin America and achieves two objectives: it highlights a programmer who uses digital tools to promote African languages and cultures within Africa itself and abroad; and it demonstrates once again that Blackness is a process comprised of history and lived experience that both taps into tradition and responds to the global possibilities created by the digital layers of culture. Adebayo is what Anna Everett characterizes as an "Afrogeek,"[19] a savvy and technologically aware African whose projects take advantage of connections available in our network society. In the interview, Adebayo acknowledges the role of digital tools in establishing connections across the African diaspora but he is also adamant that digital connections cannot take the place of person-to-person exchanges. Adebayo's brief description of his encounter with Afro-Latin America when he visited Brazil is notable in that it states both the importance of personal contacts and his surprise with a culture he thought he knew, even if only vaguely and from a distance. Although he does not elaborate more on this encounter, one can infer from his own trajectory that his experience with Afro-Latin America confirmed what he has been doing with Afro-digital tools: using their potential to establish long-distance links that also strengthen local cultures, and never forgetting that lived experience in the digital world is inextricable from the everyday experience of analog connections.

Afro-Latinx Digital Futures

Digital technologies and applications have grown exponentially, and the possibilities for expansion and collaboration to create new knowledge are being felt in a broad range of domains both inside and outside the academy. In particular, the use of digital tools in the humanities and social sciences should open up novel approaches for cross-disciplinary research and, perhaps more importantly, foster better connections between institutional and community knowledge that leads to a truly radical decolonial, intersectional, and posthuman theory and praxis in and for Afro-Latin America.

The examples in this book demonstrate that Afro-Latinx digital connections are built with a deep understanding and commitment to a diversity of lived experiences. In our contemporary era of finance capitalism, attention to the latest technological iteration and what it monetizes can blind us to the fact that technologies are for people and not the other way round. This seems like a self-evident statement, but it is clear that much discourse on technology suggests the inevitability of progress and worldwide competition for material and intellectual resources as a primary goal. However, in our time of climate crisis—and as this book is being edited, of COVID-19—we have become acutely aware that such a state of mind leads to environmental devastation and human suffering at a global scale. Colonization continues to drive governmental and corporate imperatives worldwide, with human lives secondary to economic growth. It is therefore more urgent than ever to understand and promote projects such as the ones examined in this book, projects that expand the notion of "human" by showing that Afrodescendants' agency and creativity continue to be a primary front in the struggle against a world in which elections, democracy, and discourse have been hacked to continue oppressing the many. By challenging the view that knowledge is produced in metropolitan centers and merely consumed at the periphery, those whom Johnson names deathless can teach us how digital tools could be used to transform infrastructures of death into ones for life. In this light, we hope that this is only the first of many studies of Afro-digital connections.

Notes

1. Advocates of decolonization are active in many regions of the globe, making even a summary list difficult to compile. One example of a scholar who applies a decolonial approach to Blackness is Afro-Canadian scholar George J. Sefa Dei, who has written extensively about Afrodescendant issues. See Sefa Dei, *Reframing Blackness and Black Solidarities.*

2. Intersectionality is currently an important approach in the humanities and social sciences. The term originated in a 1989 article by Kimberlé Crenshaw that examined a particular instance in which issues of race and gender needed to be addressed. See Crenshaw, "Demarginalizing the Intersection of Race and Sex."

3. As with other theoretical approaches, the practitioners are many. An example of a post-humanist examination of digital objects is Adams and Thompson, *Researching a Posthuman World*. A book-length treatise on posthumanism by one of its best-known practitioners is Braidotti, *The Posthuman*. Examples of the many practitioners who challenge anthropocentric knowledge are Bruno Latour—see Latour, *Reassembling the Social*—and Tim Ingold—see Ingold, *Being Alive*.

4. See Wynter, "Unsettling the Coloniality of Being/Power/Truth/Freedom"; see also Arriaga's chapter in this book, where the author makes reference to Sylvia Wynter and to this term in particular.

5. The terms that Michelle M. Wright uses for the historical and lived experiences of Blackness are "constructed" and "epiphenomenal," respectively. Wright, *Physics of Blackness*, 4.

6. Ibid., 8–10.

7. Ibid., 13.

8. See Castells, *The Rise of the Network Society*, vol. 1.

9. See Castells, *Networks of Outrage and Hope*.

10. See Johnson, "We are Deathless (Slavery in the Machine)."

11. María Cecilia Martino is an Argentinian anthropologist, but her ethnographic study of digital connections in the Cape Verdean community of Buenos Aires fits comfortably in the ever-evolving notion of what the digital humanities entail. For a view of digital humanities as "the next big thing," see Pannapacker, "'Big-Tent Digital Humanities, Part 1'" and "'Big-Tent Digital Humanities, Part 2'"; for a view critical of all the attention given the digital humanities, see Brennan, "The Digital-Humanities Bust"; for a view related to digital humanities from a Latinx American perspective that aims to foster dialogues between various traditions of the field, see Fernández L'Hoeste and Rodríguez, *Digital Humanities in Latin America*.

12. For example, see Posner, "What's Next"; Gallon, "Making a Case for the Black Digital Humanities"; and Fernández L'Hoeste, "Digital Humanities in Latin America."

13. For Black digital humanities, see Gallon, "Making a Case for the Black Digital Humanities"; for a postcolonial digital humanities see Risam, *New Digital Worlds*; for decolonial computing see Ali, "A Brief Introduction to Decolonial Computing"; for digital posthumanities see Hall, *Pirate Philosophy for a Digital Posthumanities*.

14. See Ortega, "Zonas de Contacto" and Aiyegbusi, "Decolonizing Digital Humanities: Africa in Perspective."

15. Monica Carrillo refers to an incident in which blackface was used on FOX Sports Radio Perú in reference to Afro-Peruvian soccer player Jefferson Farfán.

16. See Borst and Gallo González, "Narrative Constructions of Online Imagined Afro-diasporic Communities."

17. See Ng'weno, "Beyond Citizenship as We Know It."

18. Freire, *Pedagogy of Freedom*, 22.

19. Everett, *Digital Diaspora*, 157–66.

Bibliography

Adams, Catherine, and Terrie Lynn Thompson. *Researching a Posthuman World: Interviews with Digital Objects*. London: Palgrave Macmillan, 2016.

Aiyegbusi, Babalola Titilola. "Decolonizing Digital Humanities: Africa in Perspective." In

Bodies of Information, edited by Elizabeth Losh and Jacquelline Wernimont, 434–47. Minneapolis: University of Minnesota Press, 2018.

Ali, Syed Mustafa. "A Brief Introduction to Decolonial Computing." *XRDS: Crossroads, The ACM Magazine for Students* 22, no. 4 (2016): 16–21.

Borst, Julia, and Danae Gallo González. "Narrative Constructions of Online Imagined Afro-diasporic Communities in Spain and Portugal." *Open Cultural Studies* 3 (2019): 286–307.

Braidotti, Rosa. *The Posthuman*. Malden, MA: Polity Press, 2013.

Brennan, Timothy. "The Digital-Humanities Bust." *Chronicle of Higher Education*, October 15, 2017. https://www.chronicle.com/article/The-Digital-Humanities-Bust/241424.

Castells, Manuel. *Networks of Outrage and Hope: Social Movements in the Internet Age*. 2nd ed. Malden, MA: Polity Press, 2015.

———. *The Rise of the Network Society*. Vol. 1, *The Information Age: Economy, Society, and Culture*. 2nd ed. Malden, MA: Wiley-Blackwell, 2010.

Crenshaw, Kimberlé. "Demarginalizing the Intersection of Race and Sex: A Black Feminist Critique of Antidiscrimination Doctrine, Feminist Theory and Antiracist Politics." *University of Chicago Legal Forum* (1989): 139–68.

Dei, George J. Sefa. *Reframing Blackness and Black Solidarities through Anti-Colonial and Decolonial Prisms*. Cham: Springer International Publishing, 2017.

Everett, Anna. *Digital Diaspora: A Race for Cyberspace*. Albany: State University of New York Press, 2009.

Fernández L'Hoeste, Héctor, and Juan Carlos Rodríguez, eds. *Digital Humanities in Latin America*. Gainesville: University of Florida Press, 2020.

Freire, Paulo. *Pedagogy of Freedom*. Translated by Patrick Clarke. Lanham, MD: Rowman & Littlefield Publishers Inc., 1998.

Gallon, Kim. "Making a Case for the Black Digital Humanities." *Debates in the Digital Humanities 2016*. https://dhdebates.gc.cuny.edu/read/untitled/section/a22aca14–0eb0–4cc6-a622–6fee9428a357#ch03.

Hall, Gary. *Pirate Philosophy for a Digital Posthumanities*. Cambridge, MA: MIT Press, 2016.

Ingold, Tim. *Being Alive: Essays on Movement, Knowledge and Description*. London: Routledge, 2011.

Johnson, Jessica Marie. "We Are Deathless (Slavery in the Machine)." "Slavery in the Machine" issue, *Archipelagos* no. 3 (July 2019). http://archipelagosjournal.org/issue03.html.

Latour, Bruno. *Reassembling the Social: An Introduction to Actor Network Theory*. Oxford: Oxford University Press, 2005.

Nelson, Alondra, Thuy Linh N. Tu, and Alicia Headlam Hines, eds. *Technicolor: Race, Technology, and Everyday Life*. New York: New York University Press, 2001.

Ng'weno, Bettina. "Beyond Citizenship as We Know It: Race and Ethnicity in Afro-Colombian Struggles for Citizenship Equality." In *Comparative Perspectives on Afro-Latin America*, edited by Kwame Dixon and John Burdick, 156–75. Gainesville: University Press of Florida, 2012.

Ortega, Élika. "Zonas de Contacto: A Digital Humanities Ecology of Knowledges." In *Debates in the Digital Humanities 2019*, edited by Matthew Gold and Lauren Klein. Minneapolis: University of Minnesota Press, 2019. https://dhdebates.gc.cuny.edu/read/untitled-f2acf72c-a469–49d8-be35–67f9ac1e3a60/section/aeee46e3-dddc-4668-a1b3-c8983ba4d70a#ch15.

Pannapacker, William. "'Big Tent Digital Humanities,' a View from the Edge, Part 1." *Chronicle of Higher Education*, July 31, 2011. https://www.chronicle.com/article/Big-Tent-Digital-Humanities/128434.

———. "'Big Tent Digital Humanities,' a View from the Edge, Part 2." *Chronicle of Higher Education*, September 18, 2011. https://www.chronicle.com/article/Big-Tent-Digital-Humanities-a/129036.

Posner, Miriam. "What's Next: The Radical, Unrealized Potential of Digital Humanities." *Debates in the Digital Humanities 2016*. https://dhdebates.gc.cuny.edu/read/untitled/section/a22aca14-0eb0-4cc6-a622-6fee9428a357#ch03.

Risam, Roopika. *New Digital Worlds: Postcolonial Digital Humanities in Theory, Praxis, and Pedagogy*. Evanston, IL: Northwestern University Press, 2018.

Wright, Michelle M. *Physics of Blackness: Beyond the Middle Passage Epistemology*. Minneapolis: University of Minneapolis Press, 2015.

Wynter, Sylvia. "Unsettling the Coloniality of Being/Power/Truth/Freedom: Towards the Human, after Man, Its Overrepresentation—An Argument." *CR: The New Centennial Review* 3, no. 3 (2004): 257–337.

Contributors

Sandra Abd'Allah-Álvarez Ramírez, Afro-Cuban writer and activist known for her blog *Negra cubana tenía que ser.*

Adebayo Adegbembo, Nigerian computer programmer and the founder of Genii Games (http://www.geniigames.com/), which produces educational software such as the language learning program Yoruba101.

Maya Anderson-González, lecturer at Cregy-Pontois University, Paris.

Eduard Arriaga, associate professor of Spanish and comparative literature at Clark University, is the author of *Teoría Literaria* and coauthor of *Las redes del gusto: La novela en Colombia 1990–2005.*

Silvana Bahia, director of PretaLab, a maker and digital-media lab promoting the inclusion of Black women in the Brazilian field of digital technology.

Yvonne Captain, professor in the Department of Romance Languages at George Washington University, Washington, DC.

Mónica Carrillo, Peruvian poet, musician, digital visual artist, activist, scholar, and member of LUNDU, an Afro-Peruvian advocacy organization based in Lima.

Yancy Castillo and Dora Inés Vivanco from CNOA, Conferencia Nacional de Organizaciones Afrocolombianas (National Assembly of Afro-Colombian Organizations), an umbrella organization that encompasses more than 270 groups and organizations promoting and defending Afrodescendant rights and culture in Colombia.

Alí Majul, Afro-Colombian artist and activist, member of the Colectivo Contextos and Canal Cultura, Cartagena, Colombia.

María Cecilia Martino, member of the Afro-Latin American Studies Group (GEALA) at the Dr. Emilio Ravignani Institute of Argentinian and American History in the Department of Philosophy and Letters at the University of Buenos Aires and post-doctoral researcher at the National Scientific and Technical Research Council (CONICET).

Andrés Villar, writer, artist, and independent scholar.

Index

Page numbers in *italics* refer to illustrations.

Digital literacies (Alfabetizaciones digitales), 34
Digital maroonage, 28
Digital projects. *See* Afro-Latinx digital projects
Digital racialization, 27
Digital technologies and tools: access to, 8, 23, 35, 38, 46; and African indigenous cultures, 162–63; and African languages, 161–62; and Afro-Latinxs and Black digital activism, 30; and art, 90–92; and Black women, 37–39, 46–48, 50; and colonialism and colonization, 145; critical approaches to, 39; from a critical perspective, 49; as cultural artifacts, 22–23; and cultural contexts, 65–67; and cultural diversity, 47, 69–73, 160–61; and cultural education, 35; cultural effects, 2; digital divide, 23, 40n2; digital journalism, 60; and education, 54–55; effects, benefits/drawbacks of, 49–50, 58, 120, 145–46, 157; Global North/Global South divide, 23–24, 48; and human rights, 53–54; and inequality, 52–53; integration with analog tools and resources, 1, 55, 145, 156–57; and knowledge, 91–92; maker culture, 49, 52, 55; and materiality, 2–3; and mediation, 130; and physical computing, 12; racial bias in, 11; and racism, 54, 124–25, 152–53; and values, 23, 38, 39, 48; and violence, armed conflict, 121. *See also* Blogs, blogosphere; Digital domain; Digital infrastructure and support; Information and communications technologies (ICT); Internet
Directorio de Afrocubanas, 59, 60, 63, 71
Disappearance. *See* Afrodescendant visibility/invisibility; Erasure
Discrimination. *See* Afrodescendant visibility/invisibility; Erasure; Race, racism
Double consciousness, 7
Drake, Jarret, 28
Drucker, Johanna, 11, 26
Du Bois, W. E. B., 7, 166
Durban, South Africa (World Conference against Racism), 17n9, 85, 97, 132

Earhart, Amy, 13
eBlack, 10
Educafro, 99, 100–102, *114*
En 2310 y 8225, 71, 75, 76
EnCaribe, 63, 64n5
Epistemological diversity, 11, 24, 38, 39
Erasure: and Afro-Latin America, 3–4; in Colombian colonial history, 30–32; and digital humanities, 26–27; and digital technologies and tools, 11. *See also* Afrodescendant visibility/invisibility
Espinosa, Yuderkys, 75, 147
Ethnoscapes, 8, 18n18
Everett, Anna, 10, 170
Expansive consciousness, 166

Fanon, Frantz, 169
Favelas, Rio de Janeiro, 45–46, 49
Feminism in Peru, 85
Fernández, June, 75
Ford Foundation, 12, 18n33
France, 106
Freire, Paulo, 38, 55, 169
Fujimori, Alberto, 85, 95n2
Funsarep, 148, 149, 155n4

Gallon, Kim, 27, 28
Gender. *See* Afrodescendant women and digital technology; Afro-feminism; Feminism in Peru; Intersectionality; LGBTQ
General Archive of the Indies (Archivo General de Indias), 30, 31
General Secretariat for Ibero-America (SEGIB), 115n10
Gil, Alex, 62
Gilroy, Paul, 7
Global South/Global North, 23–24, 48, 166
Global Voices, 60
Gomes, Miriam, 135, 140n39
Google Maps, 33

Henken, Ted, 69
"High-Tech Couture," 49
Hines, Alicia Headlam, 10
Huellas de Africanía, 122

Reframing Media, Technology, and Culture in Latin/o America

EDITED BY HÉCTOR FERNÁNDEZ L'HOESTE AND JUAN CARLOS RODRÍGUEZ

Reframing Media, Technology, and Culture in Latin/o America explores how Latin American and Latino audiovisual (film, television, digital), musical (radio, recordings, live performances, dancing), and graphic (comics, photography, advertising) cultural practices reframe and reconfigure social, economic, and political discourses at a local, national, and global level. In addition, it looks at how information networks reshape public and private policies, and the enactment of new identities in civil society. The series also covers how different technologies have allowed and continue to allow for the construction of new ethnic spaces. It not only contemplates the interaction between new and old technologies but also how the development of brand-new technologies redefines cultural production.

Telling Migrant Stories: Latin American Diaspora in Documentary Film, edited by Esteban E. Loustaunau and Lauren E. Shaw (2018; paperback edition, 2021)

Mestizo Modernity: Race, Technology, and the Body in Postrevolutionary Mexico, by David S. Dalton (2018; first paperback edition, 2021)

The Insubordination of Photography: Documentary Practices under Chile's Dictatorship, by Ángeles Donoso Macaya (2020; first paperback edition, 2023)

Digital Humanities in Latin America, edited by Héctor Fernández L'Hoeste and Juan Carlos Rodríguez (2020; first paperback edition, 2023)

Pablo Escobar and Colombian Narcoculture, by Aldona Bialowas Pobutsky (2020; first paperback edition, 2025)

The New Brazilian Mediascape: Television Production in the Digital Streaming Age, by Eli Lee Carter (2020; first paperback edition, 2025)

Univision, Telemundo, and the Rise of Spanish-Language Television in the United States, by Craig Allen (2020; first paperback edition, 2023)

Cuba's Digital Revolution: Citizen Innovation and State Policy, edited by Ted A. Henken and Sara Garcia Santamaria (2021; first paperback edition, 2022)

Afro-Latinx Digital Connections, edited by Eduard Arriaga and Andrés Villar (2021; first paperback edition, 2025)

The Lost Cinema of Mexico: From Lucha Libre to Cine Familiar and Other Churros, edited by Olivia Cosentino and Brian Price (2022)

Neo-Authoritarian Masculinity in Brazilian Crime Film, by Jeremy Lehnen (2022; first paperback edition, 2025)

The Rise of Central American Film in the Twenty-First Century, edited by Mauricio Espinoza and Jared List (2023)

Internet, Humor, and Nation in Latin America, edited by Héctor Fernández L'Hoeste and Juan Poblete (2024)

Tropical Time Machines: Science Fiction in the Contemporary Hispanic Caribbean, by Emily A. Maguire (2024)

Digital Satire in Latin America: Online Video Humor as Hybrid Alternative Media, by Paul Alonso (2024)

Periodicals in Latin America: Interdisciplinary Approaches to Serialized Print Culture, edited by Maria Chiara D'Argenio and Claire Lindsay (2025)